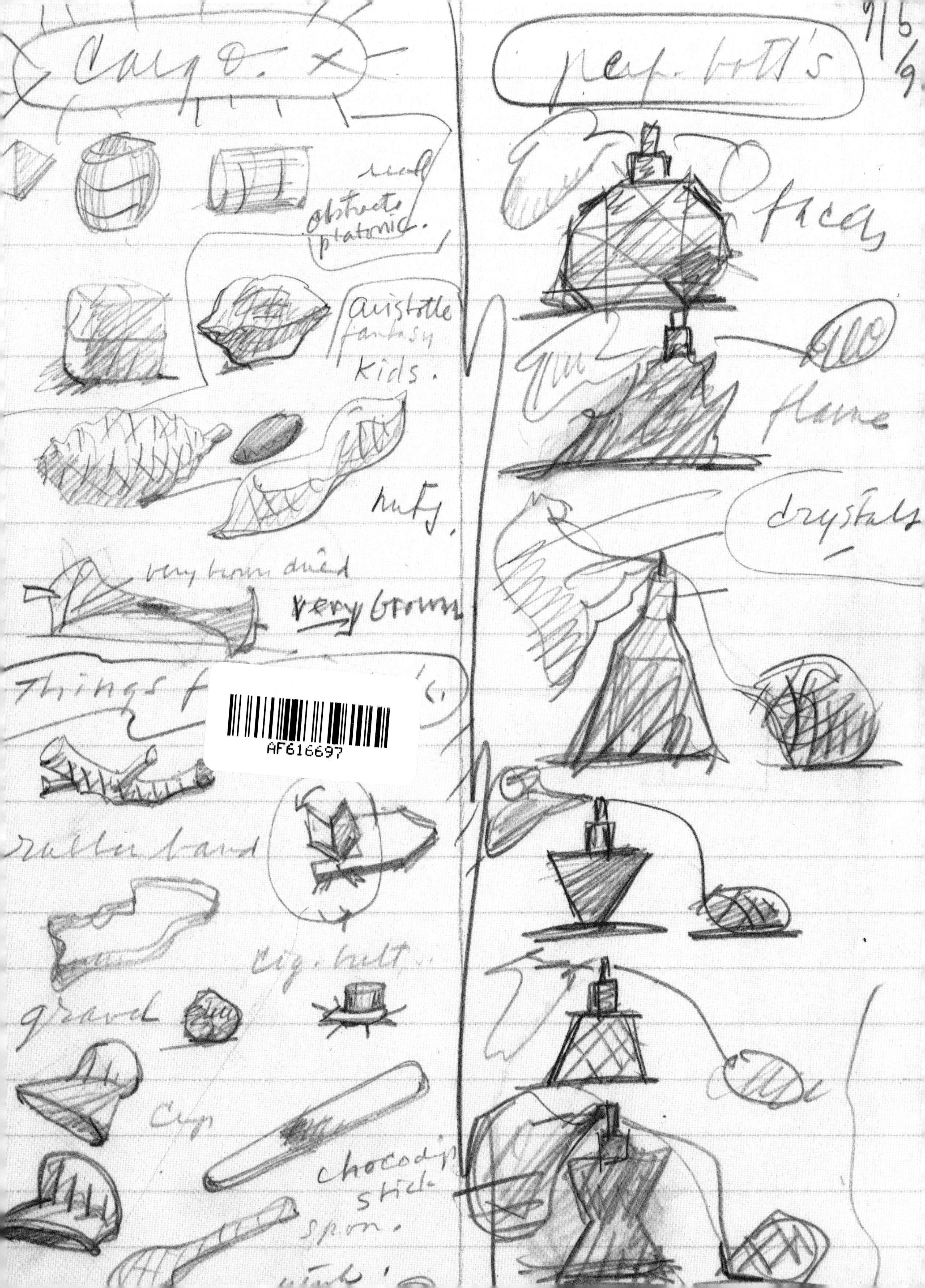

Cargo. ×

prep. bott's

9/5/9

small abstract platonic.

aristotle fantasy kids.

faces

flame

nuts.

crystals

very brown dried

very brown

Things f...

rubber band

cig. butt.

gravel

cup

chocodip stick

spoon.

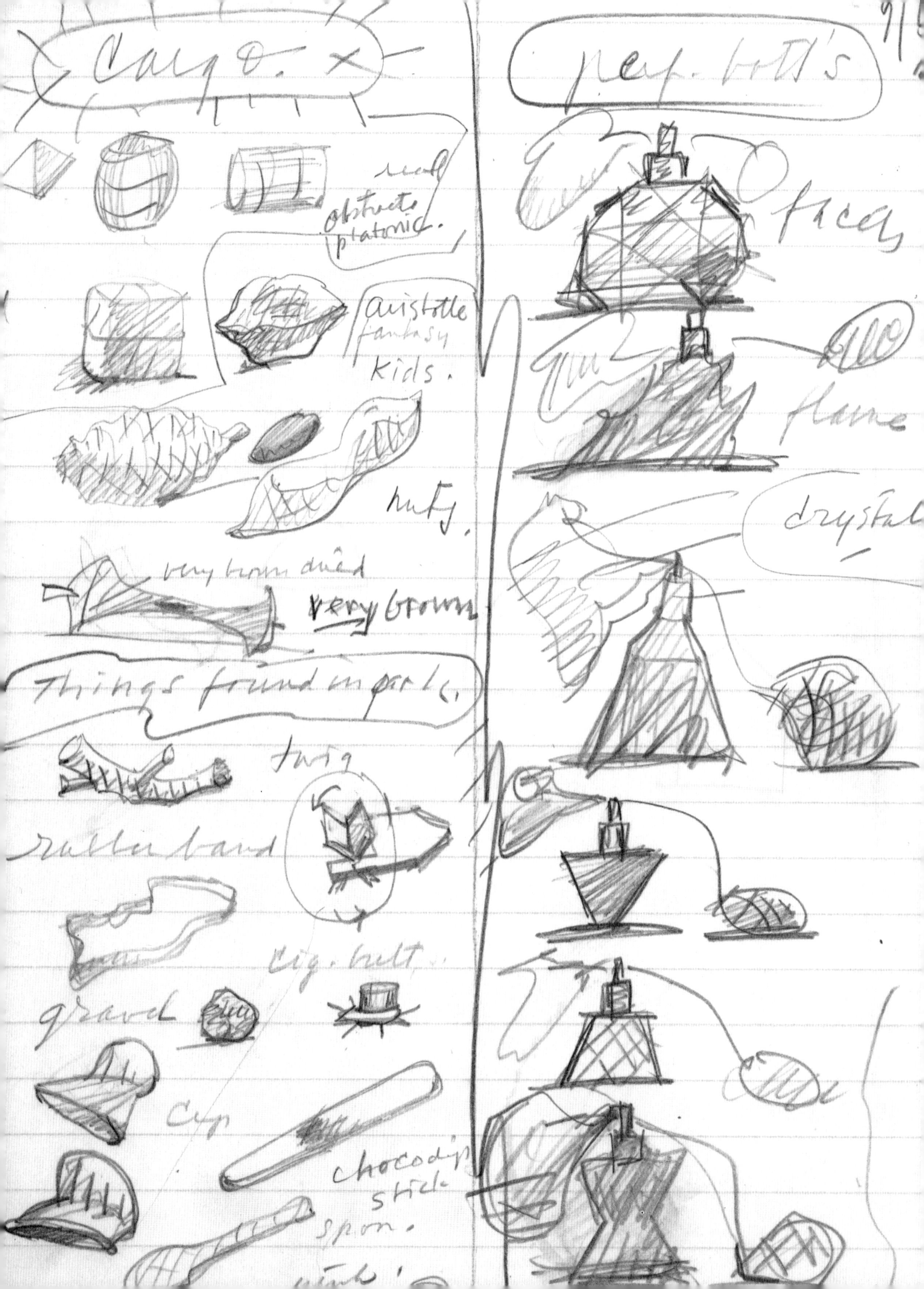

Cargo. ×

real abstract platonic.

aristotle fantasy kids.

nuts.

very brown dried

very brown

Things found in park.

twig

rubber band

big. bolt

gravel

Cup

chocodip stick

spoon.

pep. botl's

faces

flame

crystal

Claes Oldenburg

Claes Oldenburg

September 18 - October 17, 1992

The Pace Gallery
32 East 57th Street, New York City, 10022

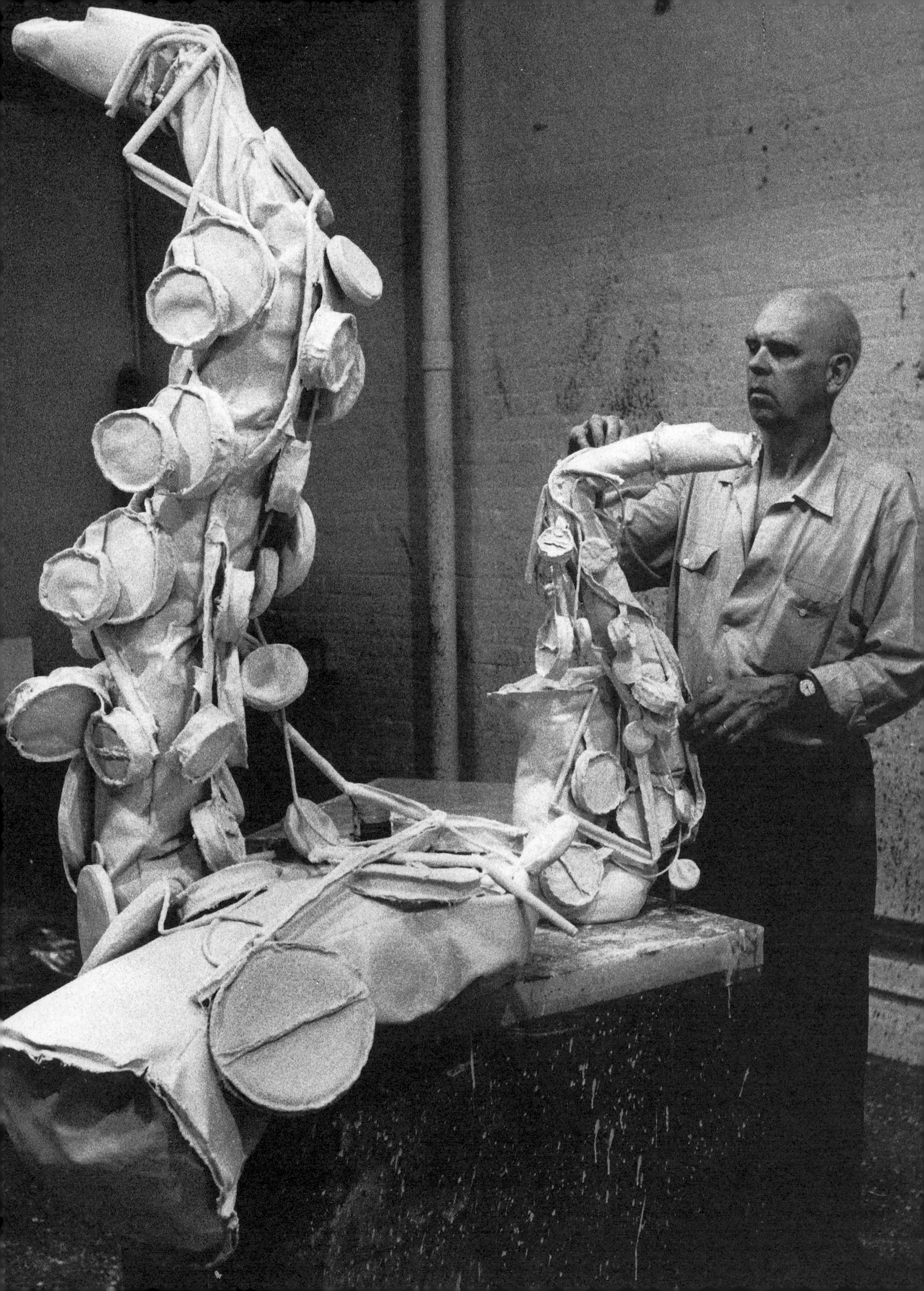

Claes Oldenburg interviewed by Arne Glimcher
July 2, 1992

Arne Glimcher:
How did objects as disparate as a harp, sax and perfume bottle come together in your mind as a sonata?

Claes Oldenburg:
Oh, I meant that the subjects are put through several variations of metaphor, and material action, changes of technique and scale, all kinds of transformations — like the melody or theme of a sonata.

Since several of the subjects are musical instruments, it seemed an appropriate analogy. The perfume bottles were in the show as well, so I just included them.

A.G.
All of the instruments and objects, including the perfume bottle, are dependent upon wind. The harp vibrates, the saxophone uses forced air, the perfume bottle's action is powered by air — in fact it creates its sound by air. Other works created at the same time, such as the *Leaf Boat* are also driven by wind.

C.O.
The soft harp, too, can stir in the air like a sail. In fact, it can be raised and lowered like a sail.

A.G.
The leaf in the boat also becomes a sail.

C.O.
In the case of the harp, the wind is very delicate, but in the case of the notebook pages — which have also become involved in the exhibition — the wind is stormy. The saxophones show a kind of twisting motion which makes one think of a spiral or tornado. And the spiral is a very important element in the notebook pages. Though torn apart, they're kept together by a spiral.

A.G.
Do the objects in this sonata have specific gender?

C.O.
This show began with thoughts circulating about certain experiences in France, where gender is an unavoidable part of an object. But gender is associated with objects everywhere,

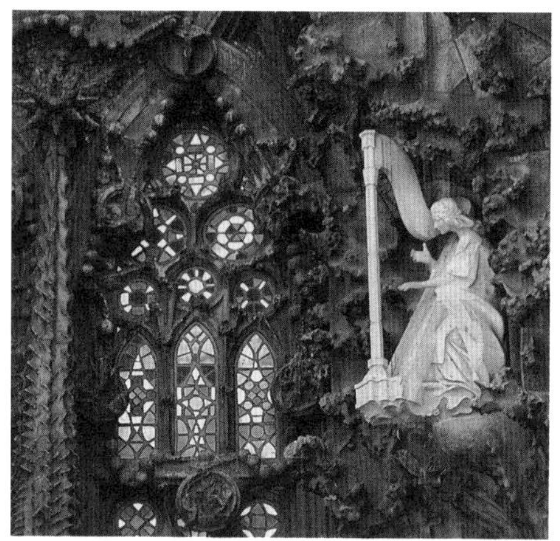

Notebook Page: *Interior of Temple de la Sagrada Familia, Barcelona, showing sculpture of harpist by Etsuro Sotoo.* postcard 4⅞ x 6¼" (detail)

such as the harp, usually shown being played by a woman, or female angel. Even Harpo Marx seems to change gender when he plays.

This can start a line of thought which, in my work, results in a combination of two or more objects in the final result. Like the literal renditions of a metaphor. The harp suggests a wing, for example, and that suggests a sail, which is confirmed by associations of women such as sirens or Lorelei playing instruments in a watery setting..

Perfume bottles tend to be more exclusively female, and some female stereotypes are invoked in developing the sculptures, like the boudoir associations of pillows or pink. The saxophone is more ambiguous. For a long time it was a man's instrument, but this is changing, and the form has a voluptuousness which I associate with a female torso.

A.G.
Your large saxophone is positioned as a seated odalisque in a decidedly seductive female pose.

C.O.
The problem is that a saxophone is always held by someone. Here it supports itself by "sitting," and the sax has something in common with a torso. The result, together with its particular scale, is rather anthropomorphic. It reminds me of *La Grande Baigneuse* by Ingres, though the "costume" is more from Delacroix.

A.G.
The reclining saxophone on brown paper, with its disconnected parts, is like a package of fish 'n chips.

C.O.
Yes, but it's a more expected position for a saxophone. Its scale is more like a real saxophone, though it's soft and therefore suggests a fish. The mantle of keys suggests a bundle of flower stems. In either case it's something which may come wrapped and has been unwrapped, hence the form of the container. The choice of cloth determines the image to a great extent: a limp saxophone feels like a fish.

A.G.
That's a very attenuated image of the saxophone, the looniest and most enormous stretch of the identity of the object in the exhibition.

C.O.
Not being a saxophone player, when I look at a saxophone,

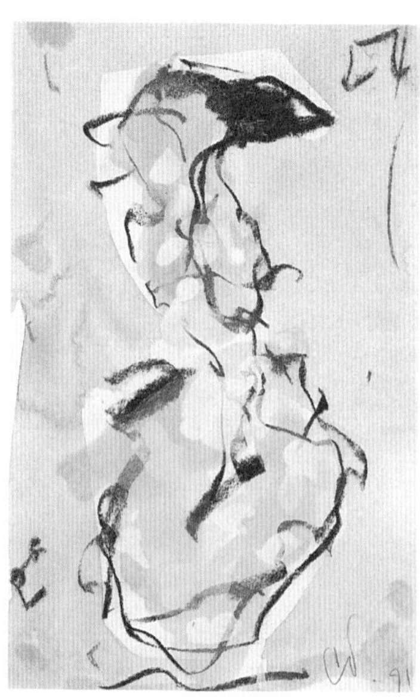

Study for Soft Saxophone, 1991
charcoal and watercolor
8½ x 5½"

I get enormously confused by the keys and valves. I represent the confusion in my version of the instrument. It's a way of de-functionalizing the object.

A.G.
Is there an underlying exercise to see how far you can attenuate this image before you lose its original identity?

C.O.
Yes. I suppose you could put the saxophone through a shredder and scatter it in the Hudson.

A.G.
You've just done it.

C.O.
I do have some drawings in which the harp is floating in water. Its softness causes it to absorb the water. It floats for a while and then sinks bit by bit.

A life cycle can be imposed on an object. An object can be very energetic and active, and then it has a dying phase and a phase of decomposition. H.C. Andersen's story of the loose collar's failed romance with a garter is like that. Coosje referred to it in an essay she was writing, and that led to the subject of the collar and tie.

A.G.
Does the point at which the object no longer has its identity fascinate you? Are you pushing the saxophone to that edge? To the point where the witch's hat disappears in the puddle in *The Wizard of Oz.*

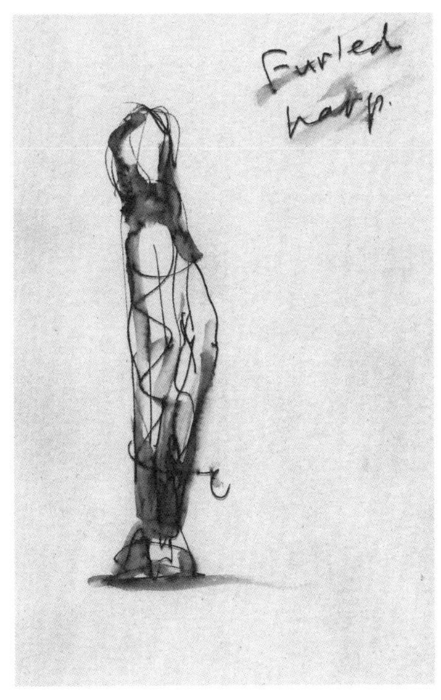

Notebook page: Furled Harp, 1992
felt pen and watercolor
5⅞ x 4¾"

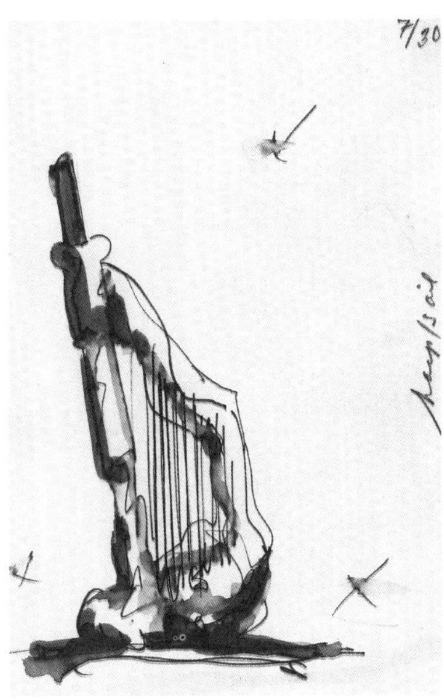

Notebook page: Study for Harp Sail, 1991
felt pen and watercolor
5⅞ x 4¾"

C.O.
It's more a matter of acquiring additional identities, but the object must hang on to its original identity in some way. Its characteristic color, for example, is never abandoned.

A.G.
There is the sense that these objects, with the exception of the *Leaf Boat,* are interior images that bring you back to the sensibility of *The Street.* During the last decade, large formal transformations of common objects often found themselves in the streets configured as sleek formal monuments. These naturally sleek objects (musical instruments, perfume bottles) have been transformed into gritty, messy street images. The saxophone seems to be dancing like a snake charmer's snake, the object of a street bazaar. Do you feel this relationship to the street?

C.O.

Yes, the scale and technique required in the fabrication of larger works doesn't favor the disheveled, detailed look of *The Street* or *The Store*, but that sensibility hasn't gone away. It was set aside in 1977 when Coosje and I decided to concentrate exclusively on large public works.

In 1984, at Coosje's urging, I returned to working in cloth and paint with the props for the performance of *Il Corso del Coltello* in Venice, Italy. This stimulated a return to intimate works and a continuation, with certain variations, of the aesthetic established in the 1960's.

The linear progression of art that had so dominated the 50's and 60's had evaporated and it was possible to do almost anything. For example, a "happening" was no longer a doctrinaire form; you could mix up "happening" ideas with commedia dell'arte and whatever. This freedom showed up in all the props which were done for the *Coltello*, with enthusiasm for the performance, without thinking a lot about art history. That attitude persisted after the performance.

A.G.

In the *Coltello* you literally come back to the street, although it was a street of water and you once again mimed the humor inherent in the objects.

C.O.

After that, the works continued in two streams: one was the large-scale projects, which Coosje and I continued to do together, and the other was the stream of more intimate, subjective, indoor work. The first manifestation was the *Haunted House* for the Museum Haus Esters in Krefeld, in 1987. The show was a metaphor for the return to the gallery in the form of throwing the objects into the museum through the window. And these objects that were thrown through the window were, of course, objects that might offend a museum. They were things found in the average suburban backyard: an apple core, a broken muffler, half of an automobile tire, totally rejected objects such as an old stuffed rabbit that nobody wanted anymore.

The *Haunted House* objects obviously have a lot in common with *The Street* objects and *The Store* objects: things that were not ordinarily to be found in museums.

A.G.

In embracing objects antithetical to those found in museums, were you engaging in another round of resuscitating discarded values?

C.O.

Well, this time around the objects had a theatrical character, either because of the *Coltello* influence or because history had made the process self-conscious. The museum, transformed into the *Haunted House*, with the famous Mies van der Rohe windows made to seem broken by the forced entry of rude objects, was a kind of set. But there was also a new thematic content: Europe, very much influenced by Coosje's vision. The important manifestations of this period took place in European museums and galleries.

In these works, the canvas became stiffened, the soft effects became frozen by the use of resins, creating a look that was soft but hard to the touch. And water-based latex was used rather than oil enamels. It was still store-bought. The approach was a bit like the house-painter's, but the palette had more white in the colors and varied from matte to gloss.

That sort of material and approach to the subject continued through *From the Entropic Library*, for the *Magiciens de la Terre* show in Paris and the *European Desk Top*, in Milan, which was a kind of reflection on the current state of Europe, and then the *Memos of a Gadfly* show in New York.

So you are absolutely right, it was a return to gritty subject matter, and also to an impure and gooey approach to material.

Something had been eaten, discarded, worn away, broken. What you experienced afterwards was a residue. Except for the *Torn Notebooks* where you're in the midst of the action and things are flying through the air. But they're headed for the wastebasket.

A.G.
In the early years of your career, the sculptures were either enameled plaster or objects made in soft canvas. The new works appear to be a hybridization of styles transmogrified through your career. As such the appearance is neither soft nor hard, brittle or malleable. In this elusiveness another aspect of metaphor in your work?

C.O.
Yes, material can either look like what it is, or something else. Cloth can be stiffened to look like metal, for example, and the result is more complicated than what you could shape or cast in metal.

A.G.
But at the same time, these stiff objects, which obviously support their own weight, look soft. From the history of your work, I assumed that the saxophone would collapse if I pushed it, the odalisque draping down over the base. It was a surprise.

C.O.
Right. It's soft but hard, which limits the possibilities. Unlike the earlier soft work where appearance was left to chance, the way that I personally prefer to have the cloth fall and the work to look — how much it sags, which way, and so on — are now fixed.

A.G.
And then the surfaces are so messy, in direct contrast to the perfect ritualized surface of the monuments. The painting is a kind of soft painting further exacerbating the contrasts. Was that deliberate?

C.O.

For me, painting is, to a large extent, gestural and textural. I like to treat paint as material — to daub it, drop it, fling it, let it slide. There was Action Painting, but I also compare it to paint effects found on the streets. This approach is superimposed on a sculptural surface which is also "painterly" with many folds that vary the way light falls on them.

A.G.

I think that these are the most elusive works you've ever made. The associations projected by the material and by the scale of the object produce radical changes in the object's demeanor. The saxophone changes from aggressive to passive, from dominant to subordinate. It reminds me of *The Sorcerer's Apprentice*, where suddenly the broom has a life of its own, and Mickey is hanging onto its coattails for dear life. Do these images develop a life of their own?

C.O.

Yes, but it's not about anthropomorphosizing, it's about releasing the many identities of forms. In animated film that happens in real time. In a sculpture, the fluctuations have to be superimposed. The sculpture should look different each time you see it, and that should keep it alive.

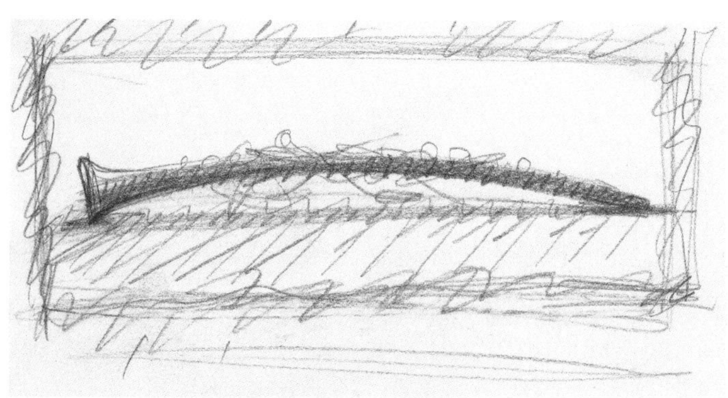

Notebook page: Study for Clarinet Bridge, 1992 (detail)
pencil
5½ x 8½"

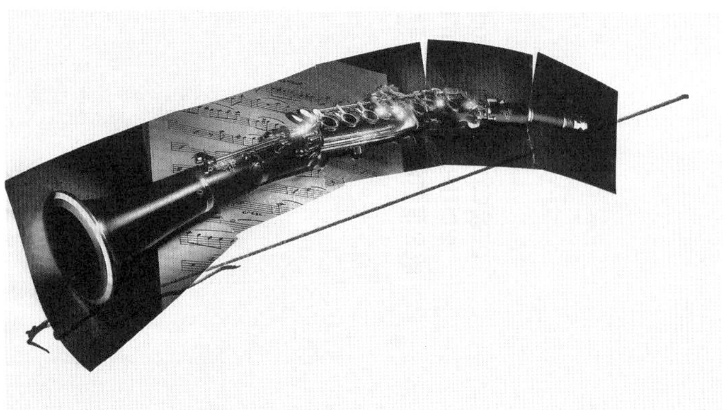
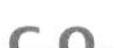

Notebook page: Study for Clarinet Bridge, 1992
felt pen and clipping
8½ x 11"

A.G.

My first impression was that these pieces referred to an earlier period of your work. Then I realized that they were the result of the entire history of your work, where images and materials transform into their opposites.

C.O.

Including our large-scale works, which usually begin as very intimate objects, like the *Mistos* (Match Cover) for Barcelona, which began at five inches and ended up 20 meters high.

A.G.

In contrast to that, the clarinet is larger than life but its metaphysical identity as a bridge conversely makes it smaller than life. How big is the clarinet?

C.O.

The clarinet is a little over eight feet long. It's arched like a bridge.

A.G.

Like the *Screwarch Bridge*?

C.O.
Yes, but not as high an arch — a low arch. More like the tusk of an elephant.

A.G.
The bridge is also like a harp, with all those vertical cables functioning as strings, holding up the bridge.

C.O.
Yes, but in these harps, the cables surrender to gravity, making the instrument useless. The clarinet resists gravity, though it was formed by hanging it upside down while the resin was applied.

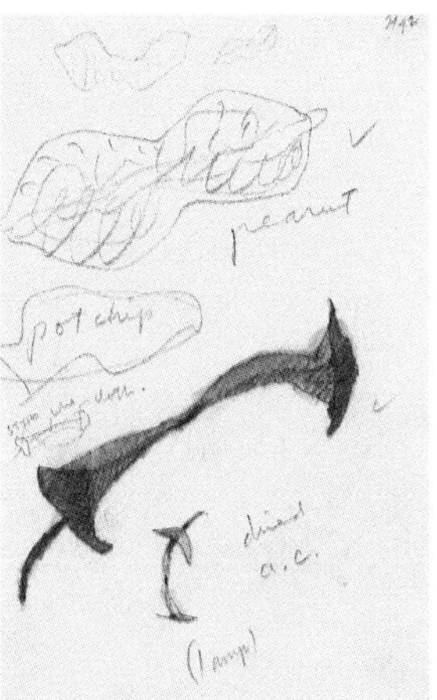

Notebook page: Study for Leaf Boat Cargo – Dried Apple Core etc., 1992
pencil and crayon
8½ x 5⅜"

A.G.
As a child in Minneapolis I used to play in the gutter with leaf boats, and float them in melting snow. Did you ever do that?

C.O.
I can't recall that I ever did, but I sympathize with the use of the most elementary means to project one's imagination. The Robinson Crusoe approach: you can create art out of almost anything. In that sense, the *Leaf Boat* is related to the *Street Doll* made of rags and wire for *The Street.*

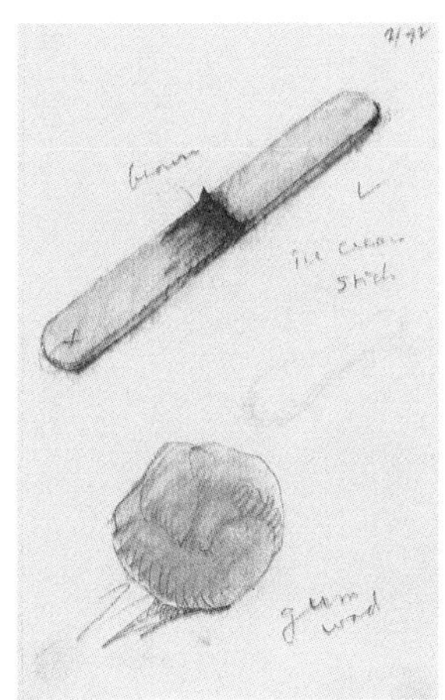

Notebook page: Study for Leaf Boat Cargo – Ice Cream Stick and Gum Wad, 1992
pencil and crayon
8½ x 5⅜"

When Coosje and I visited the Calder place in Saché, France, in 1990, I looked on the ground for some kind of souvenir. The only thing I could find was a little piece of cardboard cut like the top of a picket fence. It was sort of a sign for a house, and I took it home and placed it on a shelf with other objects. It eventually led to the *Leaf Boat* subject, or its revival — years before I had drawn it as a sculpture in the Rhine, tied up at Basel.

A.G.
Your *Leaf Boat* radically changes its scale. This is a tiny intimate object that becomes elephantine. It is, however, still smaller than the *Raft of the Medusa* that inspired its construction.

C.O.
Usually a subject oscillates between several scale identifications. One is the *Leaf Boat* as built by a child, a primitive structure, as in the model. Another is the scale of a human-sized boat, which is the scale of the sculpture. Then there is an imaginary scale, as you say, an echo of the *Raft of the Medusa* by Gericault. It's as if, after visiting the painting in the Louvre, one devised a frivolous version out of scraps found in the gardens of the Tuileries. The *Leaf Boat* is loaded with a cargo of bottle caps, peanut shells, ice cream sticks, wads of gum and whatever is lying around, and sailed out on the pools of water there.

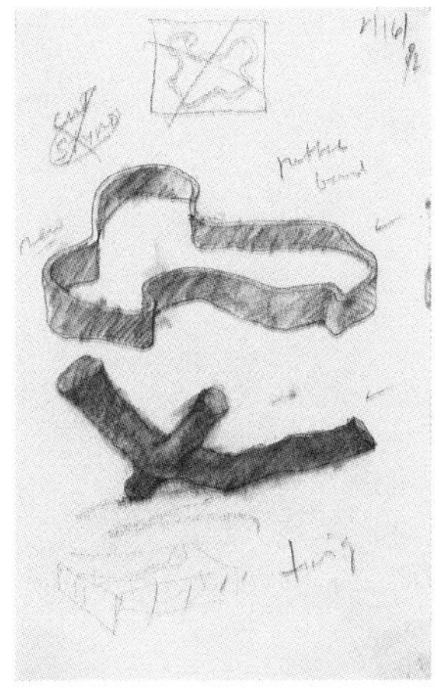

Notebook page: Study for Leaf Boat Cargo – Rubber Band and Twig, 1992
pencil and crayon
8½ x 5⅜"

A.G.
Are these fragments or scraps also metaphors for what becomes of the people on the *Raft of the Medusa*?

C.O.
They become larger than life in the gallery scale and might be stand-ins, in a remote sort of way.

A.G.
But your "raft" is almost minimalist, in contrast to the construction of the *Raft of the Medusa.*

C.O.
Yes, what primarily interests me is the position of the "raft": the relation between the tilted plane and the wall and the resulting situation of the "leaf." The simplicity of the subject helps. It's an exercise in reduction, taking the most emotionally charged painting I know.

Coosje points out that the *Leaf Boat* has something in common with earlier minimalist-style works like the *Lingerie Counter*, or *The Bedroom Ensemble*, which emphasize geometric forms and angles, and location in a space, as well as a hot subject coolly reduced. The *Lingerie Counter*, also had a mast (two, in fact) with different kinds of underwear — more organic forms, also stiffened like the "leaf" suspended on them.

Movement and texture are most important to me, but there is always an underlying architecture. Now and then, that becomes more exposed. In the large-scale projects, for practical reasons as well, it is a dominating element.

The final result of the *Leaf Boat* might be in yet another scale, a large version on the axis of the Tuileries, on end, as if breasting a wave, but without the wall, to play off the obelisk or some other pyramid in the vicinity.

A.G.
Or I.M. Pei's pyramid.

C.O.
Yes, Pei's pyramid would be a good foil.

A.G.
The notebooks are created by the impulsive act of tearing them apart. How do impulsive accidents figure in other images?

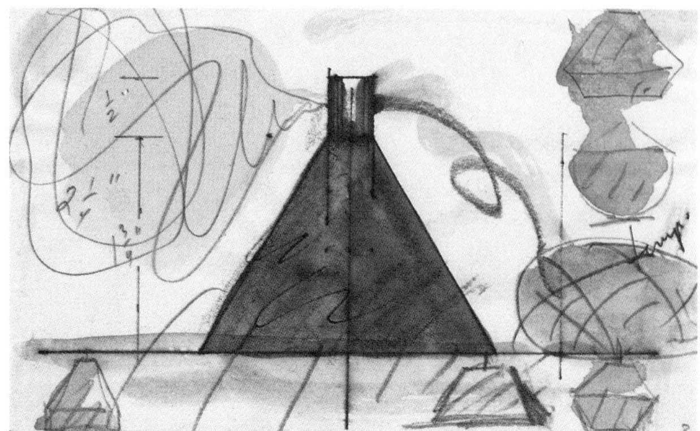

Notebook page: Study for a Sculpture in the form of a Perfume Bottle, 1991
felt pen, pencil and watercolor
3⅝ x 6"

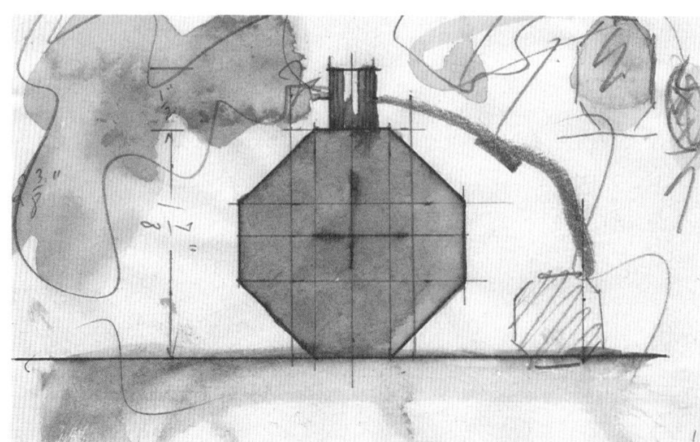

Notebook page: Study for a Sculpture in the form of a Perfume Bottle, 1991
felt pen, pencil and watercolor
3⅝ x 6"

C.O.

The fallen perfume bottle, maybe. There are two situations for the *Perfume Bottles.* One is hieratic, standing on a shelf, sphinx-like. The forms are inflated but flat, as in relief. They're fixed to the shelf, and the only thing they're doing is inflating or leaning slightly in the direction of the "pouf."

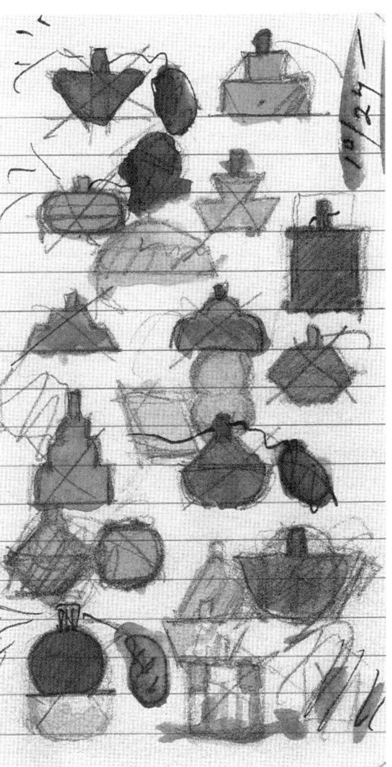

Notebook page: Various Shapes of Perfume Bottles, 1991
pencil and watercolor
5 x 2¾"

The other is the fallen version, which shows the aftermath of having fallen or being thrown.

A.G.

For that you need a domestic argument in the mix, don't you?

C.O.

Or maybe it just fell off the shelf.

Perfume is a rich subject, but I think I've perversely steered away from its identity, at least in the rigid ones. They're just geometrical forms, three similar but discrete forms together, softened and lined up like sculptures on a pediment. They're clumsy with jagged connections which contradict the elegance of most bottles of perfume. The form of the cloud of fragrance is as solid as the other two elements, or as a vinyl-covered cushion. The fringe on the bulb is vestigial.

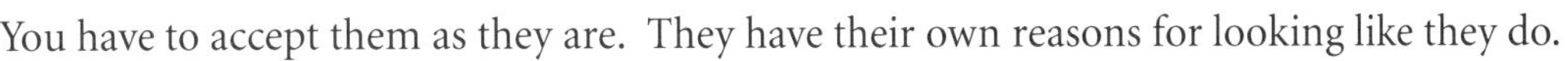

You have to accept them as they are. They have their own reasons for looking like they do.

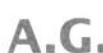

A.G.

I have a funny association with them. There's a movie called *The Thing.* The Thing monster was a giant vegetable, a carrot or something.

C.O.

I remember that movie very well, yes.

A.G.

The scientist saves some seeds from the giant carrot and plants them in a greenhouse. The seeds grow producing little breathing lungs. The "pouf" of the perfume bottles looks just like those lungs from *The Thing.*

C.O.

But this has nothing to do with that. The forms result from the material chosen, and from staying within a shallow plane. I admit the result is surprisingly visceral, and the function of forcing air is like the lungs.

A.G.

You've painted the standing perfume bottles to look ephemeral and soft, but the material is hard and seems at odds with the object.

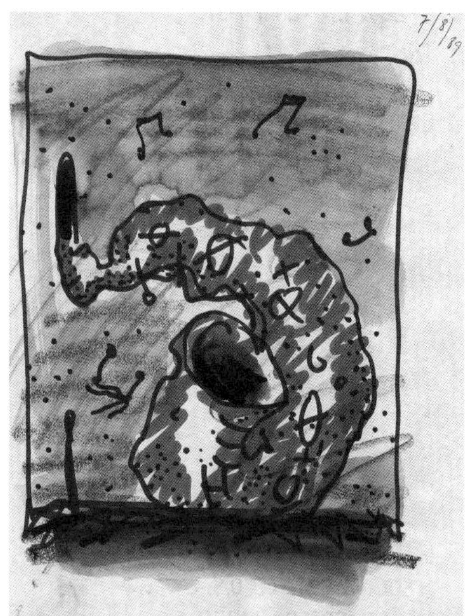

Notebook page: *Soft Saxophone*, 1989
felt pen, crayon and watercolor
11 x 8½"

C.O.

Yes, it's watery and glazelike — that does have something in common with perfume. It tries to dematerialize the solids by creating a kind of atmospheric landscape.

A.G.

You're legendary as a great draftsman. Unlike you, most of your generation of artists became draftsman late in their careers. Learning how to draw was like on-the-job training, as drawing was not the major concern of the image-makers of your generation or the generation of Abstract Expressionists before you.

How much do you have to fight this facility that is not typical of your peers? You can make anything look like art. Is there a conscious battle going on for you to strip the drawing of facility?

C.O.

It's very hard to define drawing. For example, I find it almost impossible to obtain a likeness. My drawing seems to be the projection of a world inside me, shaped by gestures naturally produced by my body. I censor the work not in the doing so much, but in discarding what I don't like. Facility can be all right, if it fits. Every drawing has its own rules.

Drawing should be uninhibited. Some may be art, some may just lead to art, some may not be art at all and still be interesting. I think of Picasso's remark that if he were locked in a prison cell without any tools, he would be compelled to draw in the dust on the floor with this tongue.

A.G.

Picasso also drew with a flashlight.

C.O.

Well, you could say everything that moves leaves a "drawing," like a slug, or the vectors of a cab making its way up Sixth Avenue. People I have never seen draw on the front of our building at night.

A.G.

But you just painted away the graffiti on the front of your building.

C.O.

For many years we let it accumulate as a kind of history: the earliest entry said "Vote for Goldwater." Recently our neighbors began to feel very threatened by it, and we gave in to their request to paint it over. But the history will probably resume.

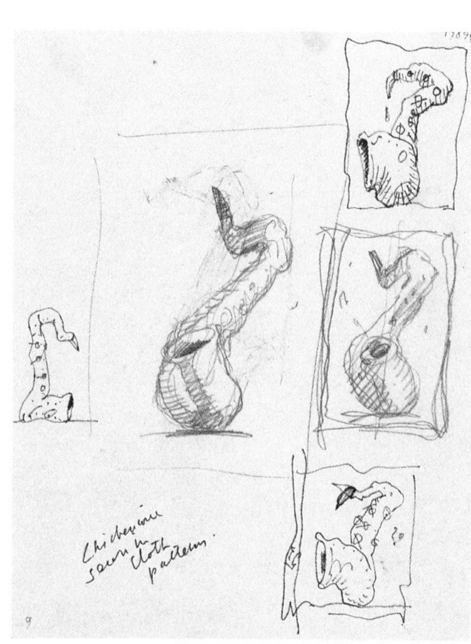

Notebook page: *Study for a sculpture in the form of Soft Saxophone*, 1989
pencil
11 x 8½"

A.G.

Have you seen the Clouzot film on Picasso?

C.O.

No.

A.G.

In it Picasso is drawing on the back of thin paper with a marker, so that the image comes through. The camera is underneath the paper. And he begins, a squiggle starts, and it's a very weird thing because you have absolutely no idea what image he's creating. By the end of the drawing, there's an extraordinary classical odalisque sitting on the page. He began the drawing with her fingers and it grew organically. It's an amazing thing, like watching the realization of a pre-conscious model happening from any single point within it. Do your drawings start like that?

C.O.

When someone is watching, you tend to come up with an image you know well. In my case, perhaps that would be an apple core rather than a nude, and certainly nothing classical. But fresh drawing is another matter: it's much too revealing. I have to do it alone.

A.G.

Your drawings take place before, during and after the completion of the work. Are the drawings part of the process of transforming these images?

C.O.

Certainly. The drawings begin on a very small scale as the setting down of an idea.

A.G.

Are they made in a notebook?

C.O.

The notebooks are the place where all my ideas appear at first. The procedure with the notebooks is that every two weeks, whenever they're filled, I go through them and take out the things that seem worth developing. I glue these up on 8 1/2 x 11 inch sheets and I put them in a binder. The remaining notebook is torn in half and discarded, which produces the form that is used as the basis for the *Torn Notebooks*.

A.G.

Do you save the torn notebooks?

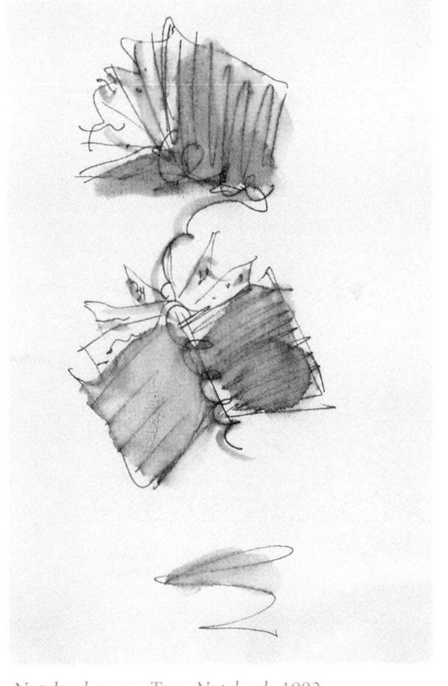

Notebook page: Torn Notebook, 1992
felt pen
8½ x 5½"

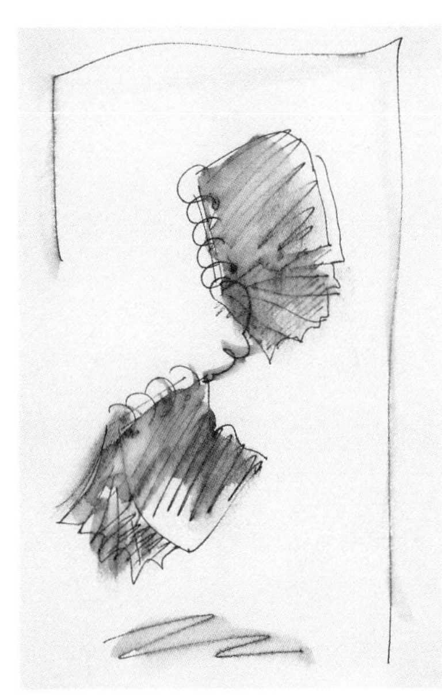

Notebook page: Torn Notebook, 1992
felt pen
8½ x 5½"

C.O.
Not until I started to appreciate them as possible sculptures. And then I saved a few and mounted them for study.

A.G.
Perhaps we should install the show so that you enter through the notebooks. First, the actual notebooks ripped open, then the sculptures of notebooks, then the objects from the notebooks.

C.O.
Yes. But the notebooks seen by themselves are also kind of a frightening image of a whole torn in half and then just clinging together by the spiral. Or two separate parts in tenuous connection.

A.G.
Like dreams and reality?

C.O.
Yes, or the tension between opposites.

So that's how it starts, these notes are gathered. After that there are different kinds of larger drawings. There's a sort of architectural, schematic drawing which enables me to get the subject to the proper scale and ultimately leads to the construction of the sculpture. And then there's another kind of drawing which is an end in itself. It has an illustrational character to it because it's really a drawing of the sculpture. As with the *Leaf Boat*, it's a drawing of the sculpture in different contexts, such as floating in the sea.

A.G.
Does the sculpture then serve as a model for the drawings?

C.O.
Yes, for the situations depicted in the drawings.

A.G.
So the saxophone as odalisque could then become a model to draw from, not unlike life drawing?

C.O.
The sculpture itself becomes the subject in the later stages of a theme. These drawings can be rough, impressionistic, or carried to a high degree of finish if they're going to be posters or prints. The subject may be repeated many times in variations until it fades out.

A.G.

The three drawings of the leaf boats are not unlike taking the saxophone to the fish 'n chips stage. The image is attenuated to the point where it is almost lost, like the drawings of the torn notebook, where it's hard to recognize the identity of the image. There's just a little squiggling explosion on the page — a violent scribble.

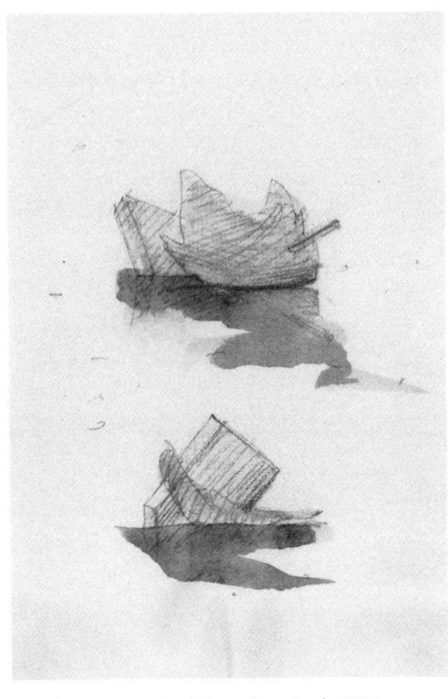

Notebook page: Leaf Boat, Capsized, 1992
pencil and watercolor
8½ x 5½"

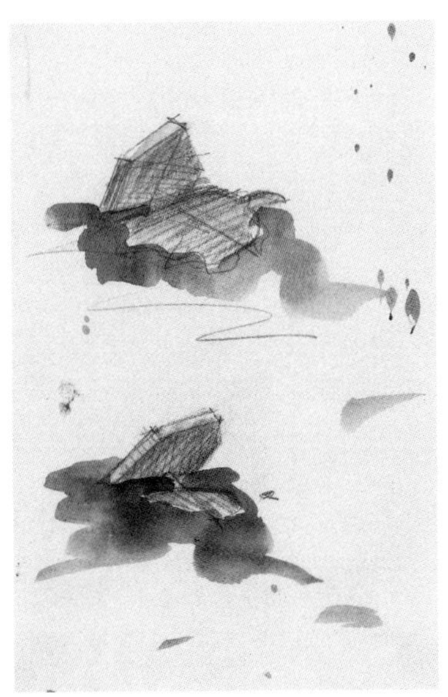

Notebook page: Leaf Boat, Capsized, 1992
pencil and watercolor
8½ x 5½"

C.O.

If you're feeling explosive, drawing is the perfect medium. Besides, one of the ways to create a sensation of space is to explode something in that space and have the fragments fly all over it, giving you a sense of distances.

But there are also drawings of the same notebook subject that are very calm. They vary from explosion and tearing to a silent, winged effect.

A.G.

Does chance play a role in the physical process of the drawing? When you apply paint to the sculpture, the dripping and splattering can take the character in other directions. Can it also transform the process of drawing and, ultimately, sculpture?

C.O.

Oh sure — by relaxing muscles, letting gravity take over, watching things accumulate, letting nature go its way. I equate art with weather, or forces in the street. Every day in front of my house there's a new landscape of spilled and running things in odd relations.

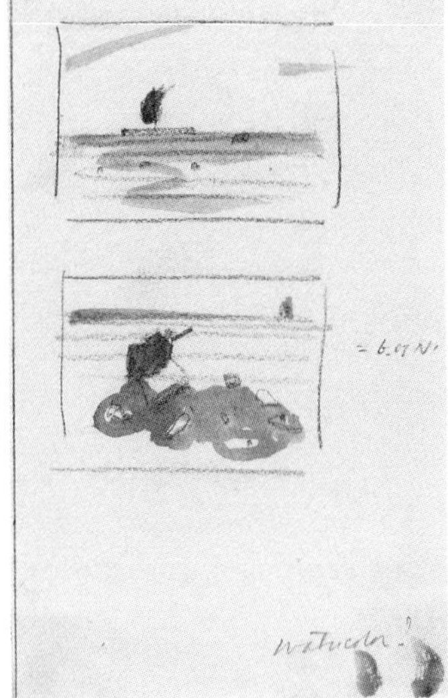

Notebook page: Leaf Boat, Becalmed, with Cargo, 1992
pencil and watercolor
8½ x 5⅜"

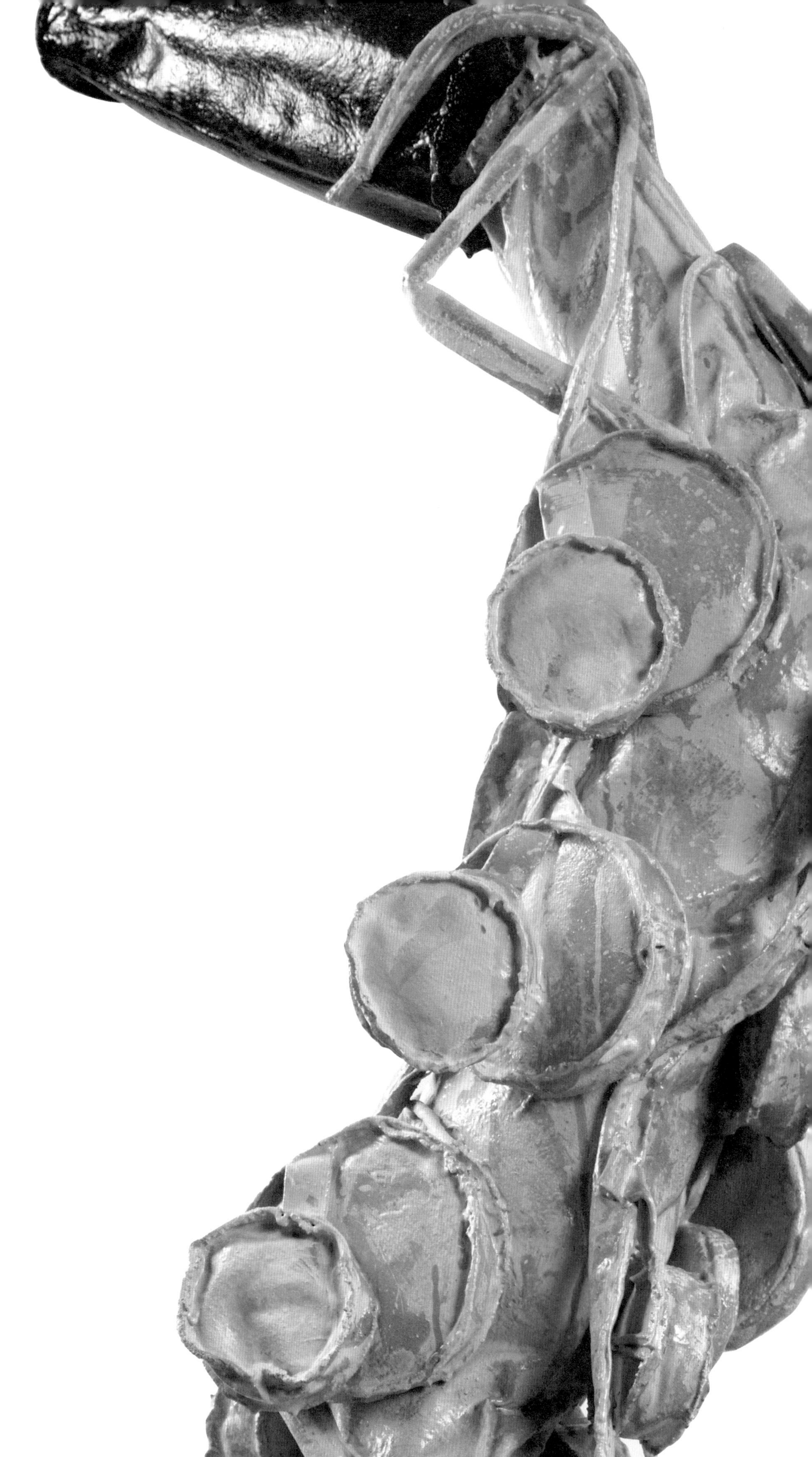

Soft Saxophone, Scale A, 1992
muslin, wood, clothesline, dacron, resin and latex paint
32 x 12½ x 15"

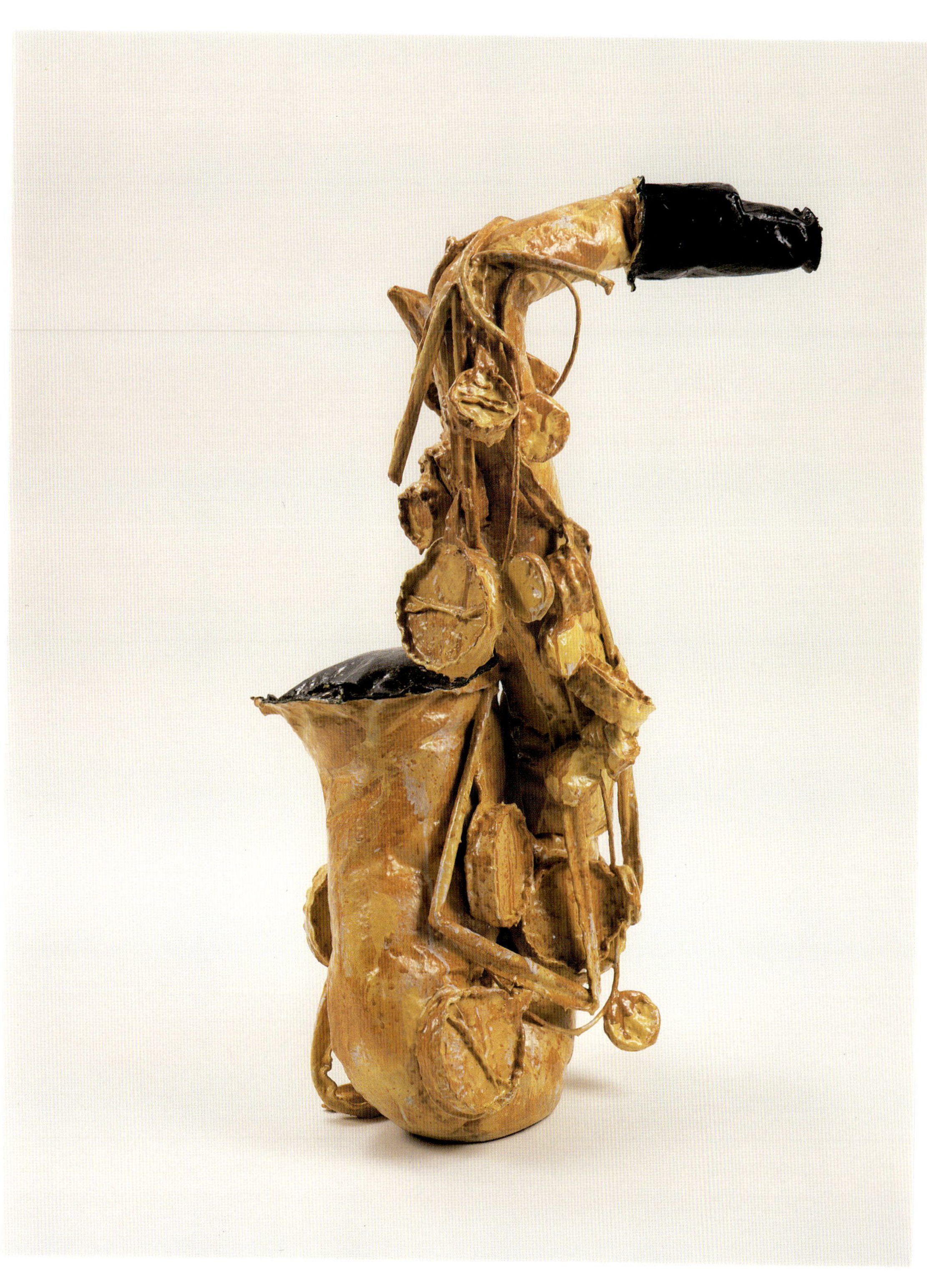

Soft Saxophone, Scale A, Vinyl, 1992
vinyl, urethane foam and wood
38½" attached to ½ x 24 x 24" base

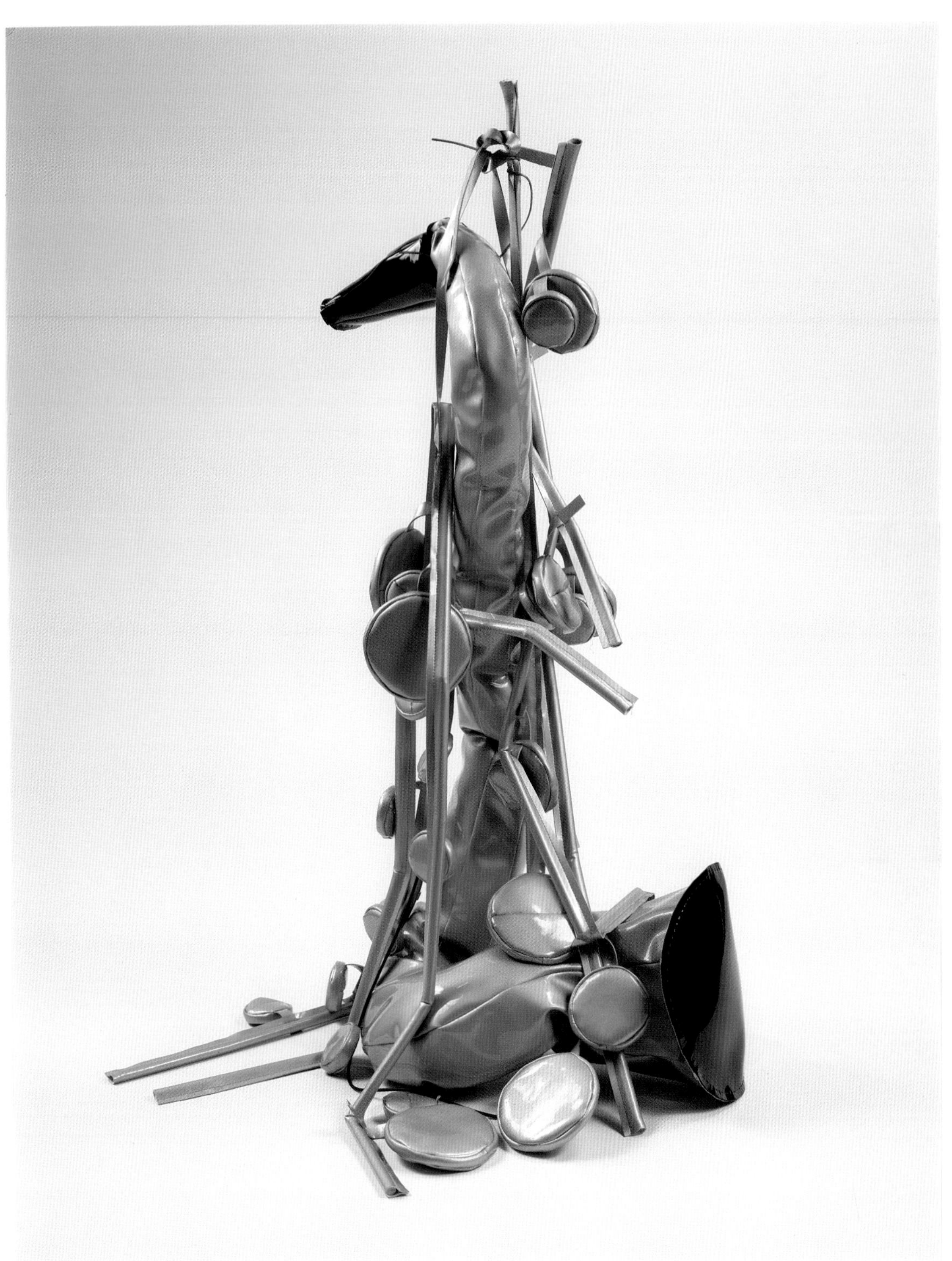

Soft Saxophone, Scale A, Muslin, 1992
muslin, hardware cloth, urethane foam, wood, dacron and latex paint
11 1/4 x 27 x 49"

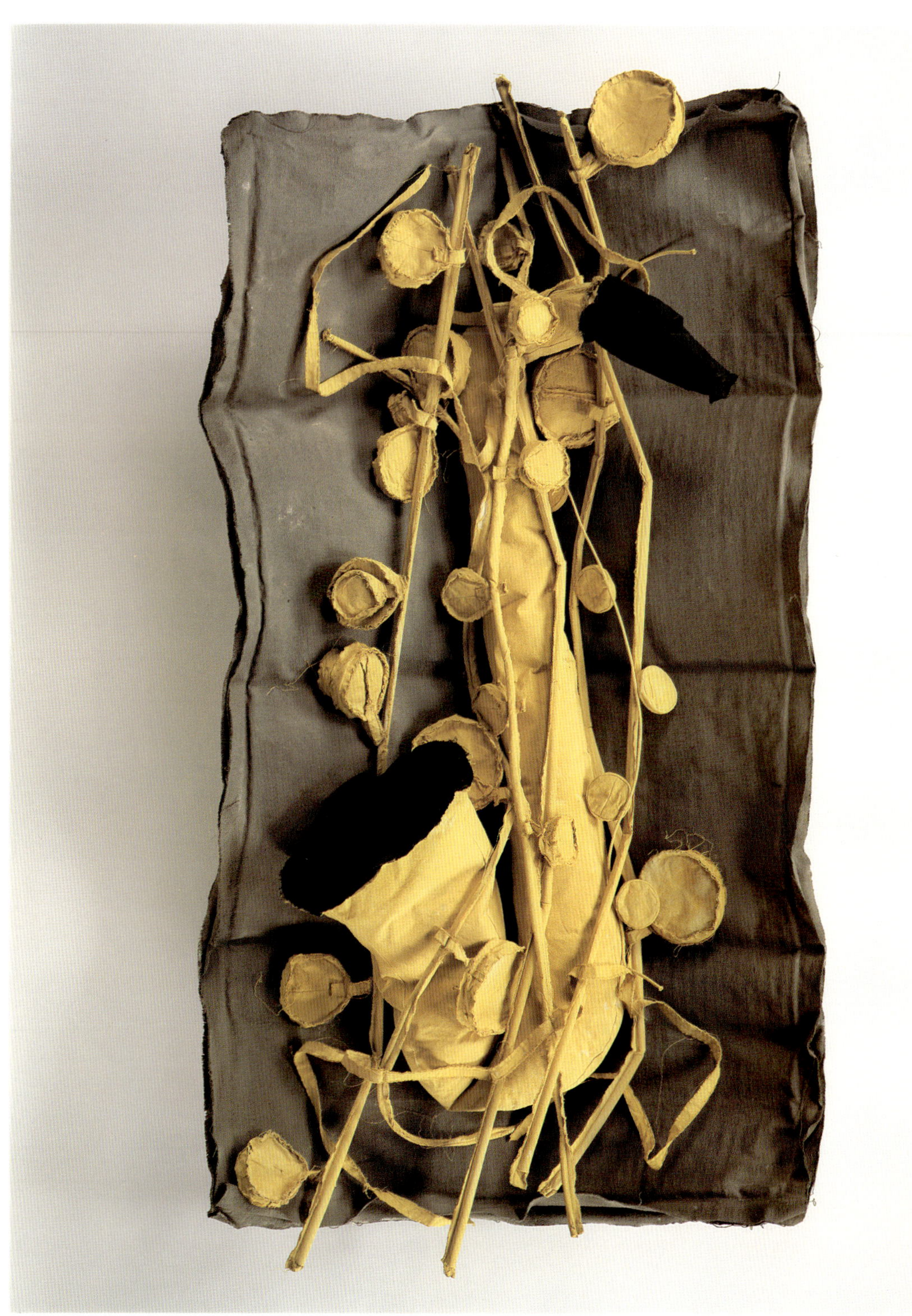

Soft Saxophone, Scale B, 1992
canvas, wood, clothesline, dacron, resin and latex paint
69 x 35 x 36"

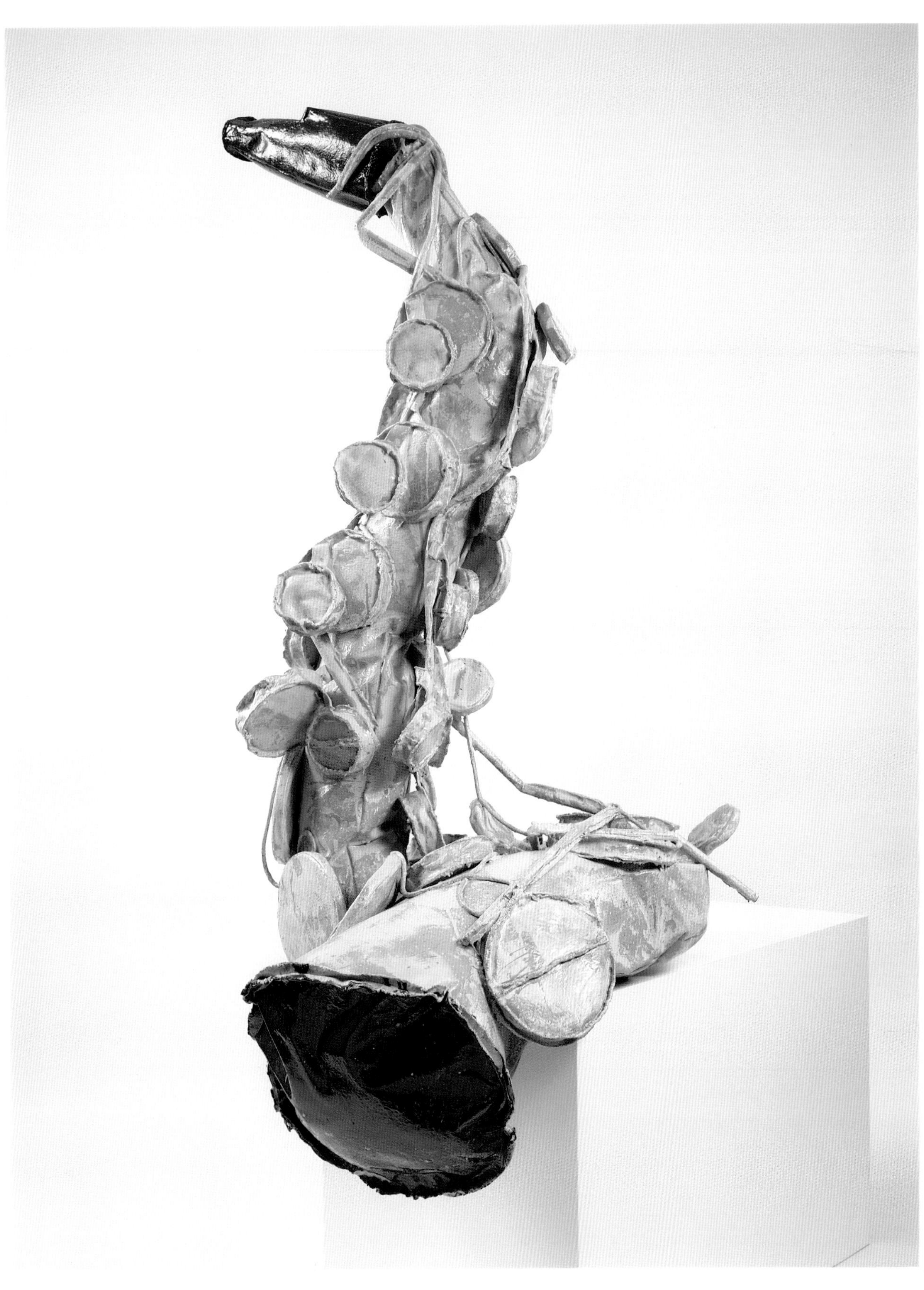

Soft Harp, Scale A, 1992
muslin, steel, clothesline, dacron, resin and latex paint
51 1/2 x 27 x 7 1/2"

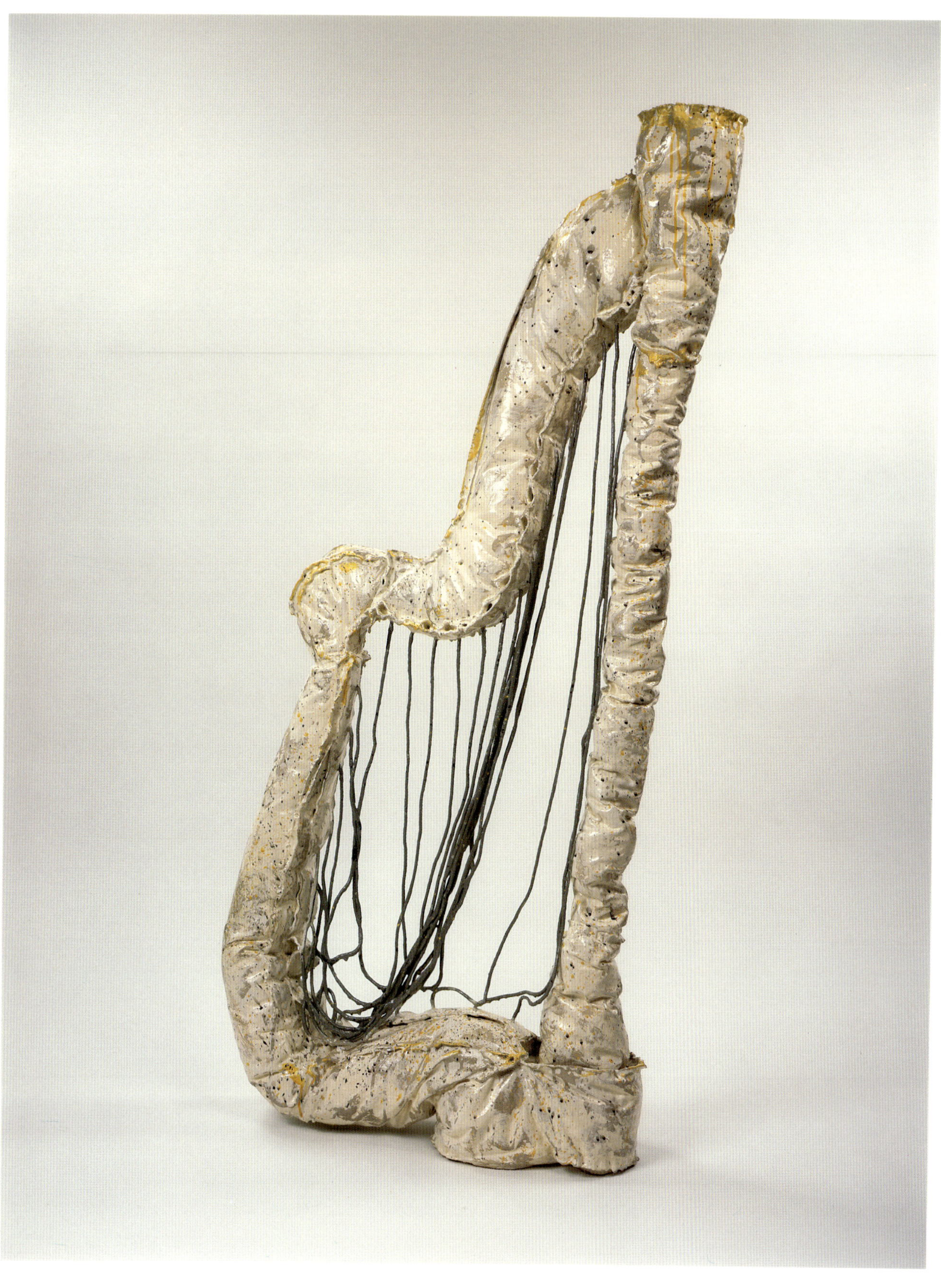

32

Soft Harp, Scale A, Harp Sail, 1992
muslin, dacron, sash cord, wood, aluminum and latex paint
65 1/2 x 8 x 27" attached to 1 x 12 x 27" aluminum and wood base

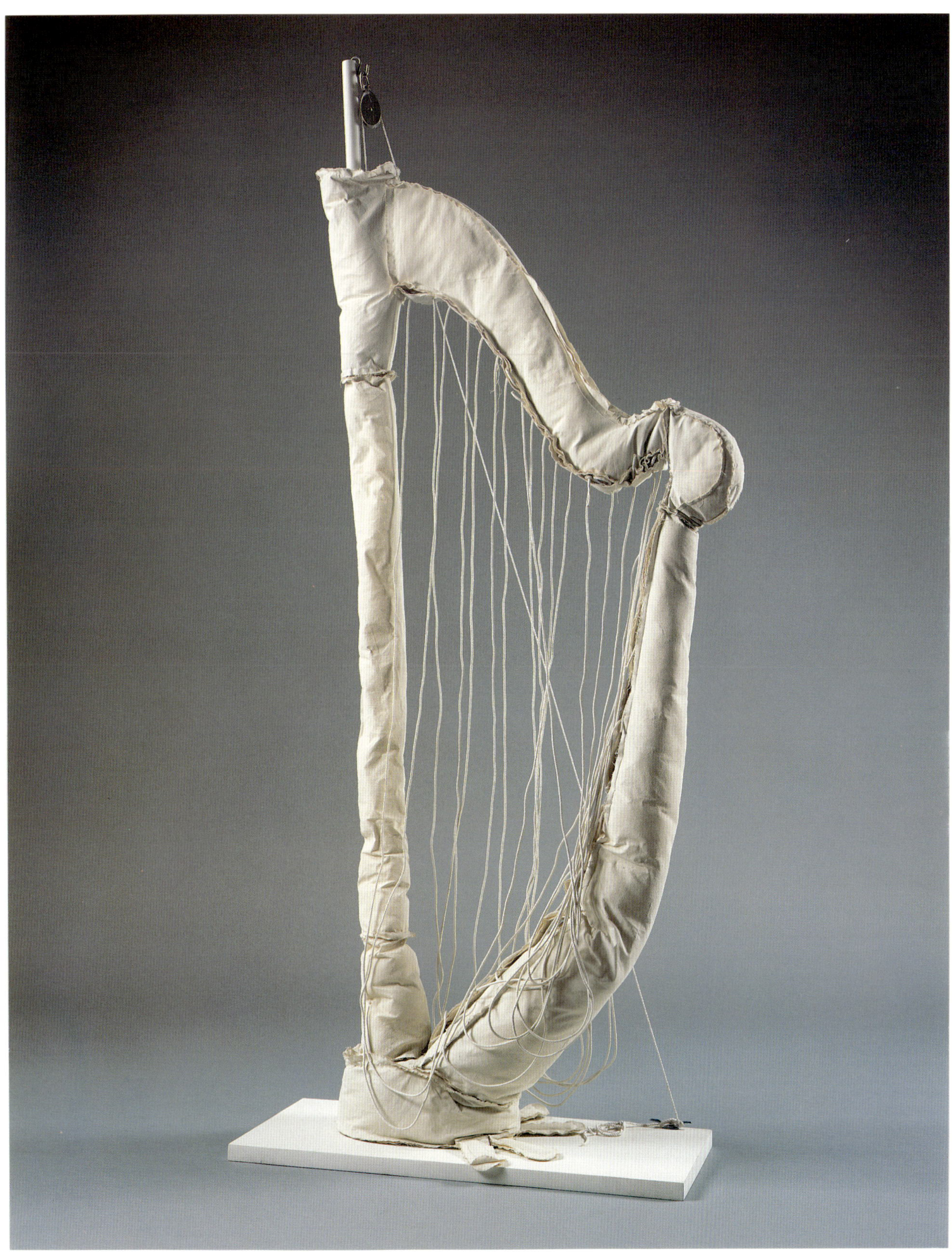

Soft Harp, Scale A, Harp Sail, 1992, (Lowered)
muslin, dacron, sash cord, wood, aluminum and latex paint
65 1/2 x 8 x 27" attached to 1 x 12 x 27" aluminum and wood base

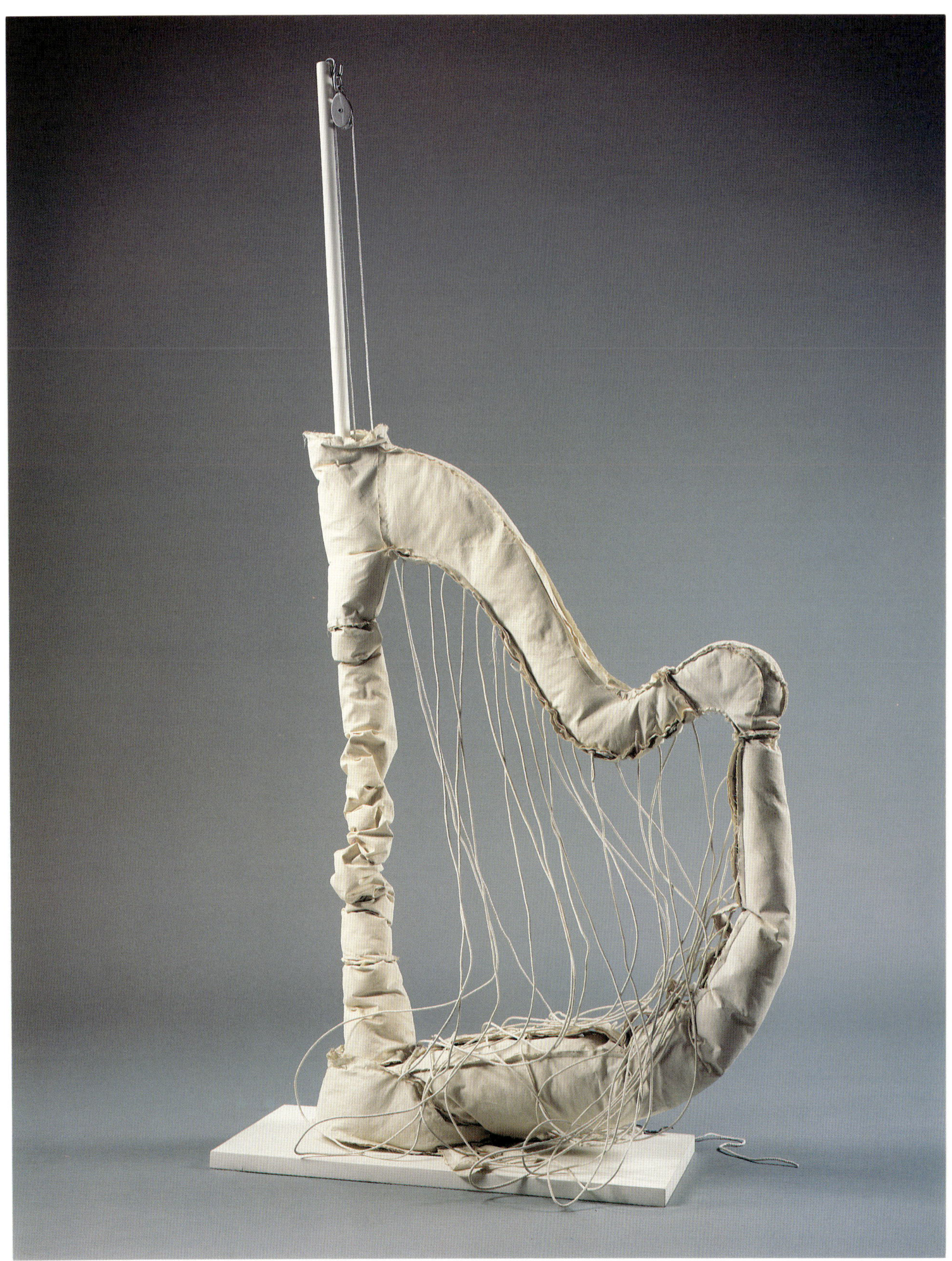

Soft Harp, Scale B, Ghost Harp, 1992
canvas, steel, aluminum, clothesline, expanded polystyrene, dacron and latex paint
95 x 27 x 48"

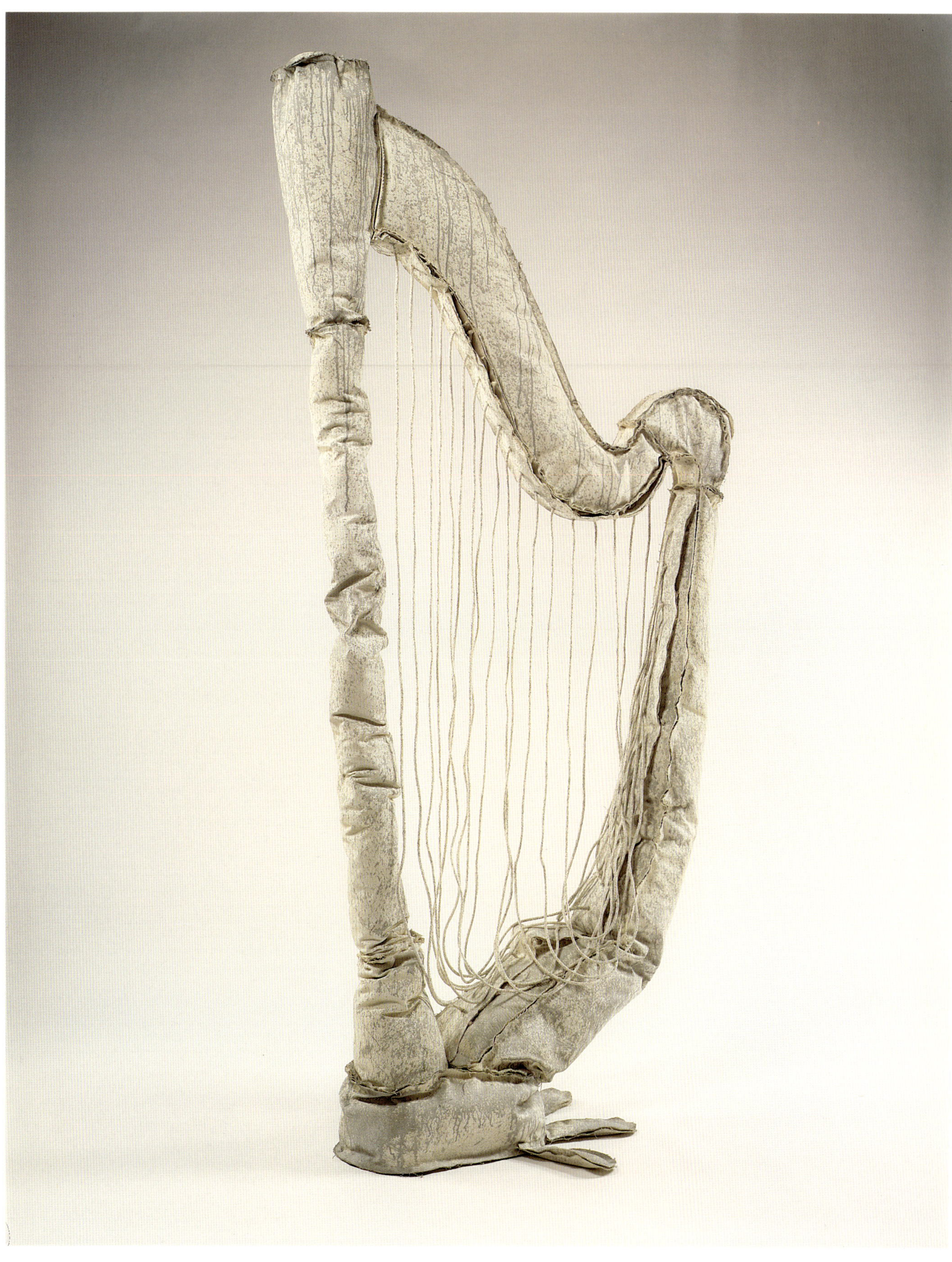

Soft Harp, Scale C, Harp Sail, 1992
wood, steel, aluminum, clothesline, feathers and latex paint
98 x 24 x 123½"

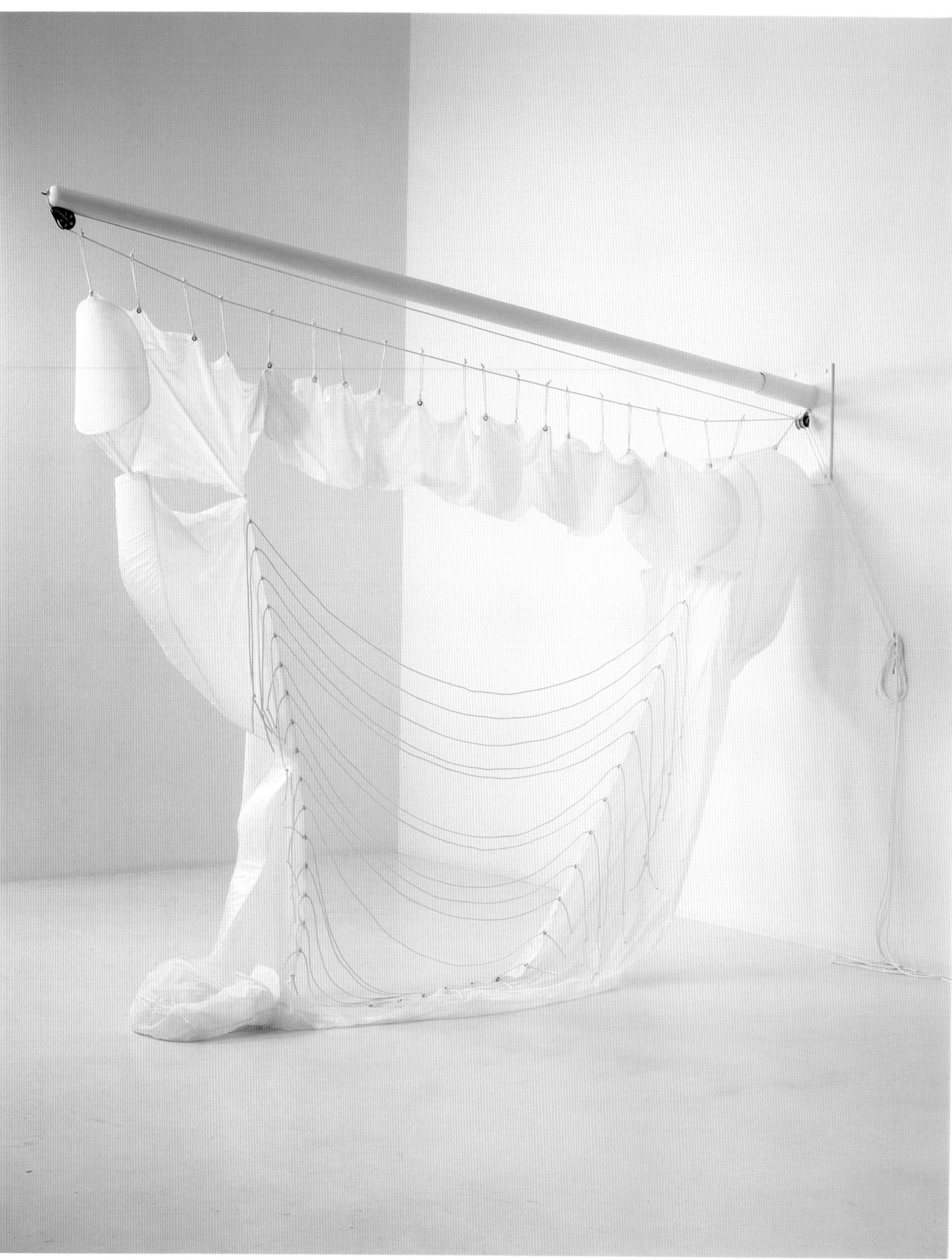

Clarinet Bridge, 1992
canvas, wood, clothesline, urethane foam, resin and latex paint
14½ x 11¼ x 98"

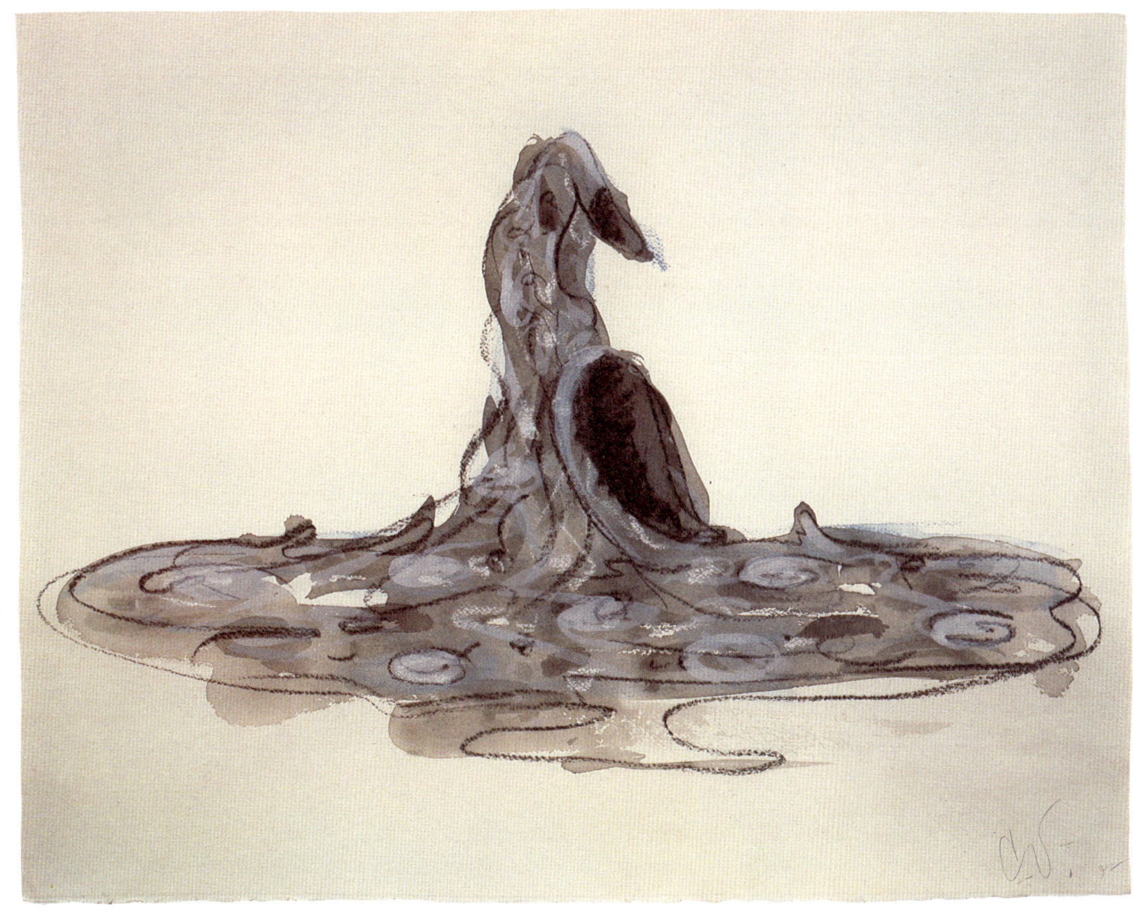

Saxophone Fountain, 1992
charcoal, crayon and watercolor
20 x 26"

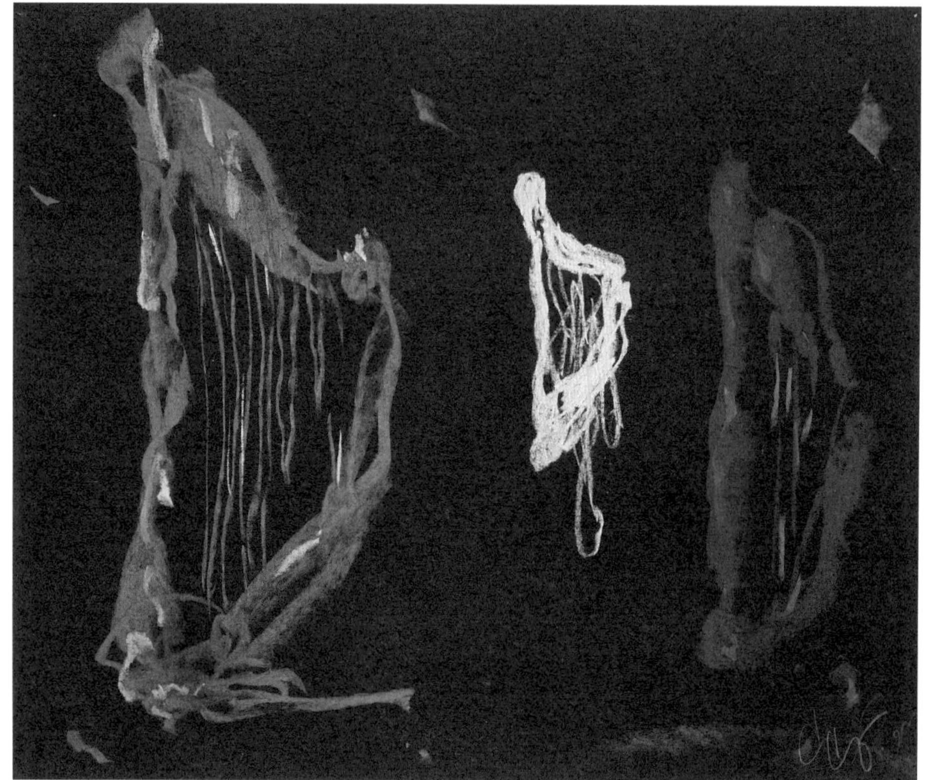

Harps in Séance, 1992
pastel
14 x 17"

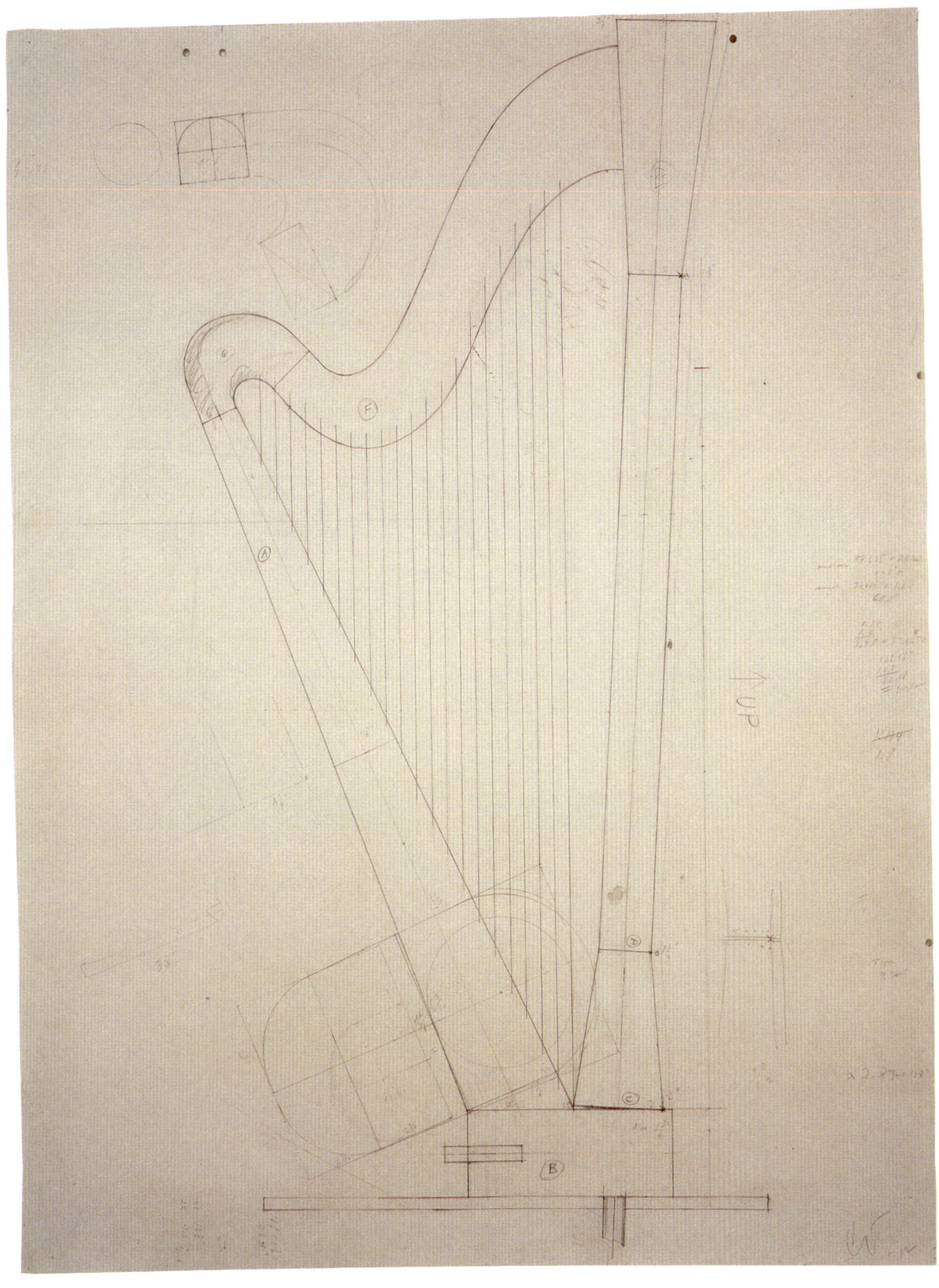

Soft Harp, Plan, 1992
pencil
40 x 30"

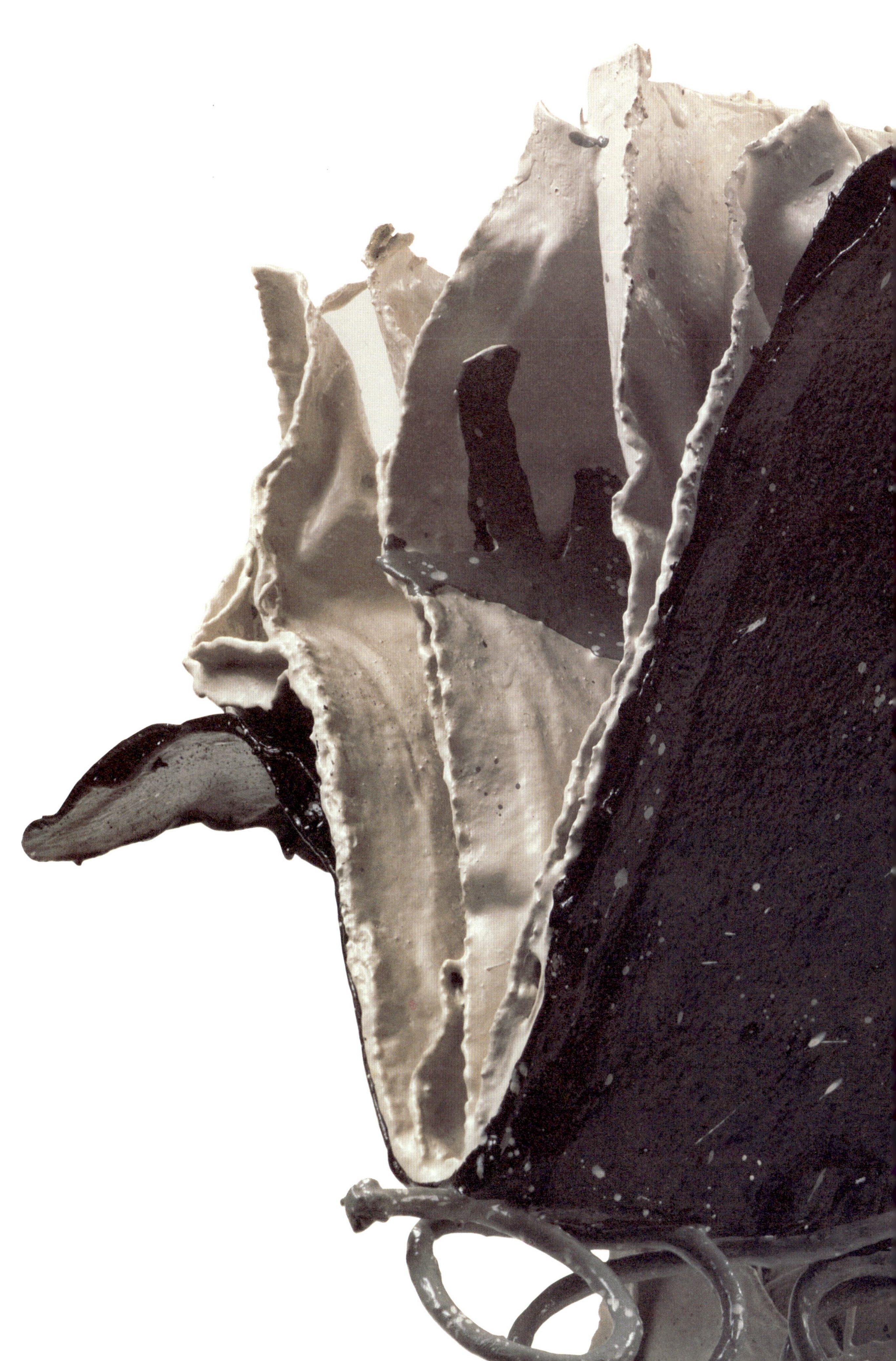

Torn Notebook, One, 1992
muslin, chicken wire, clothesline, steel, resin, and latex paint
24 x 25 x 19" attached to 1/2 x 24 x 24" aluminum plate

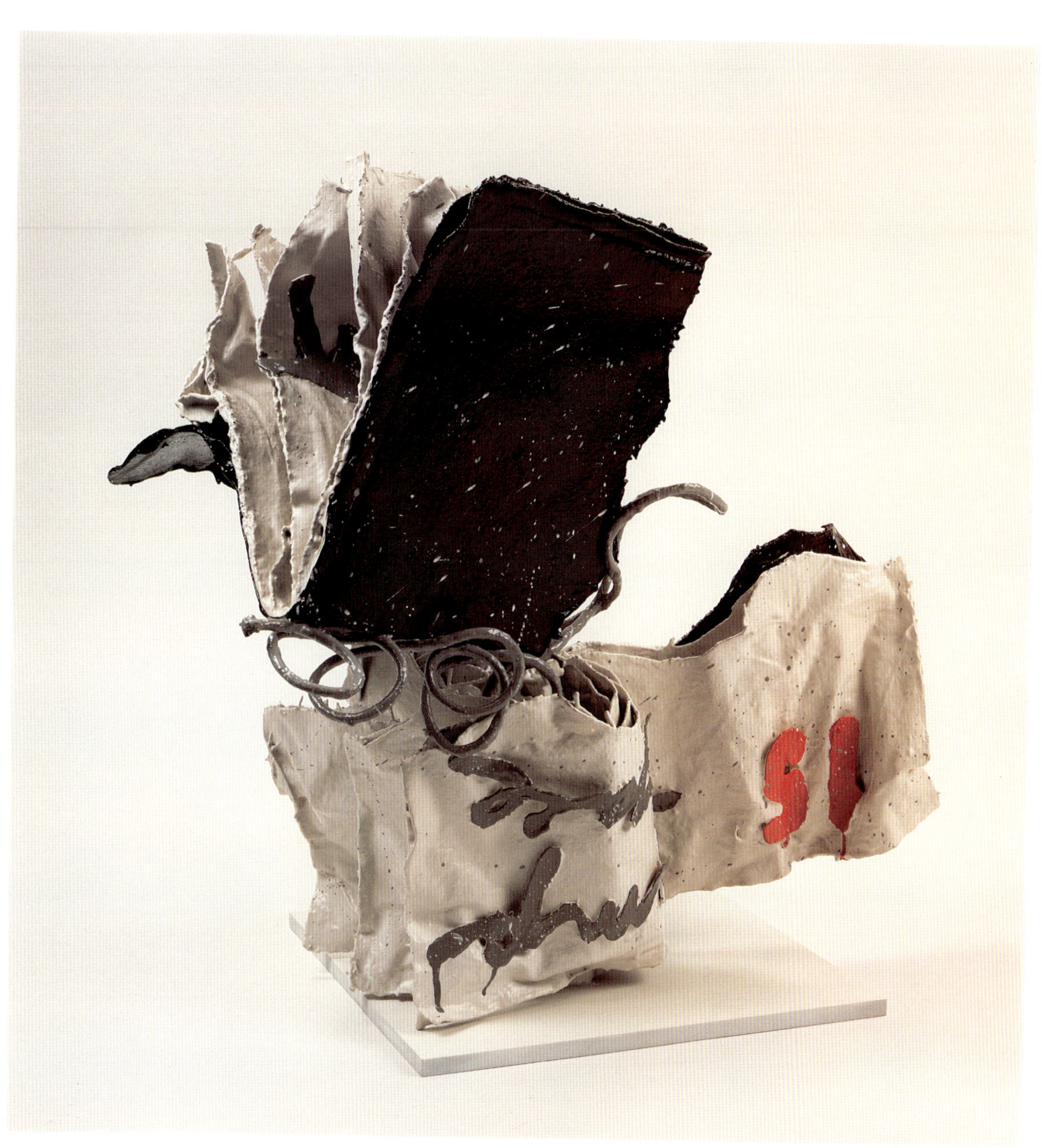
SI

50

Torn Notebook, Two, 1992
muslin, chicken wire, clothesline, steel, resin and latex paint
30 x 24½ x 24" attached to ½ x 12 x 12" painted aluminum plate

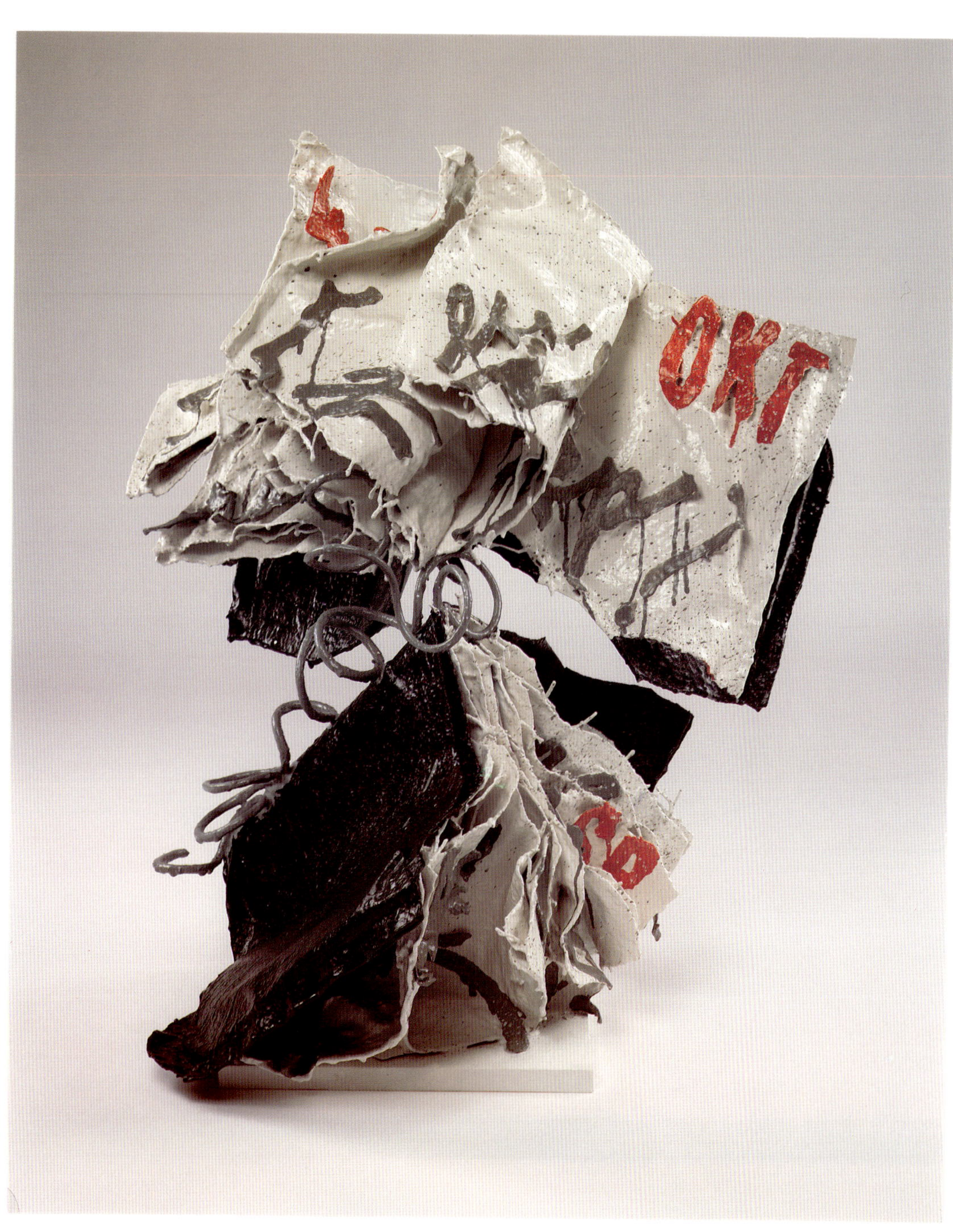
OKT

52

Torn Notebook, Three, 1992
muslin, chicken wire, clothesline, steel, resin and latex paint
24 x 33 x 36" attached to 1/2 x 8 1/4 x 8 1/4" aluminum plate

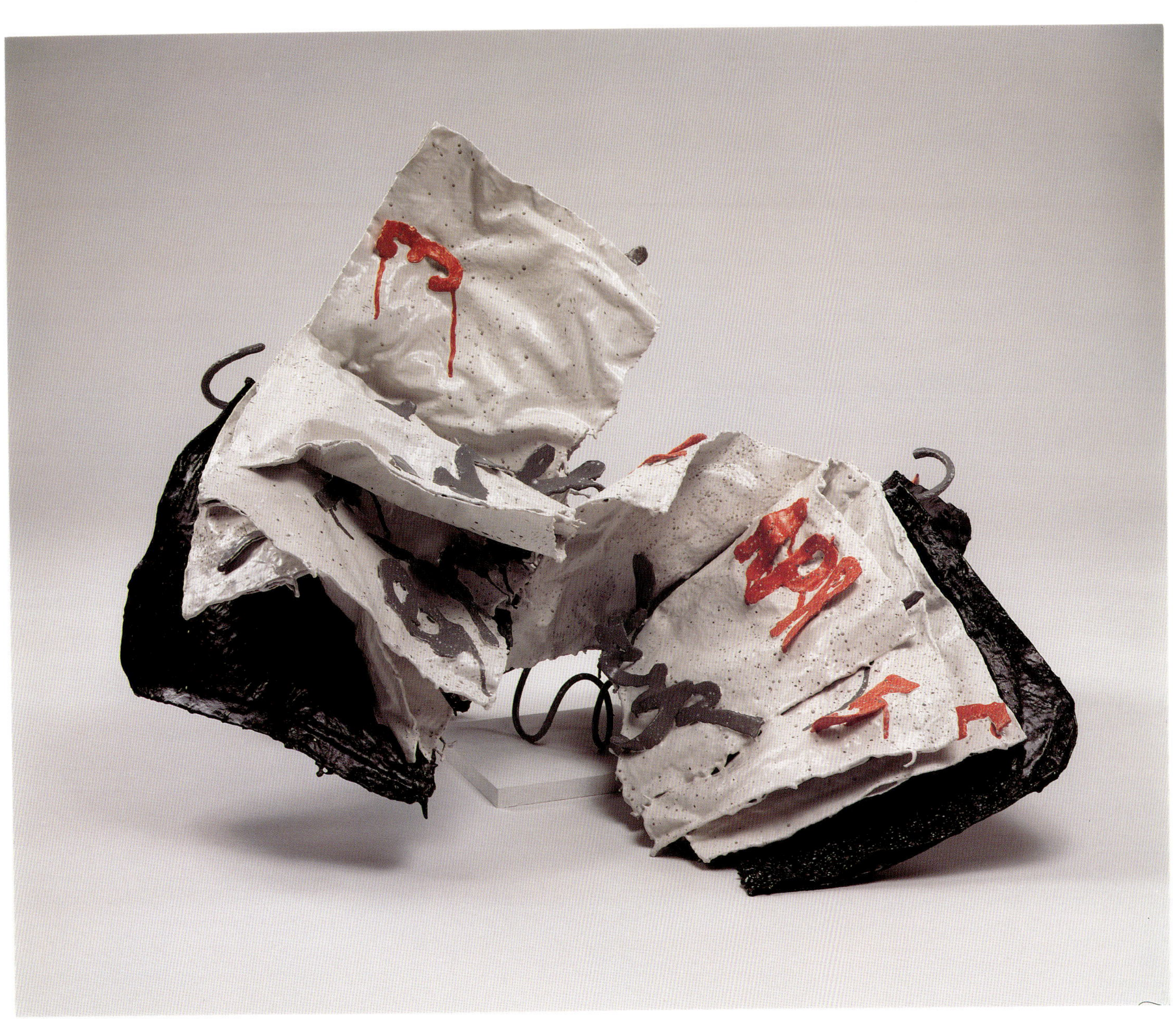

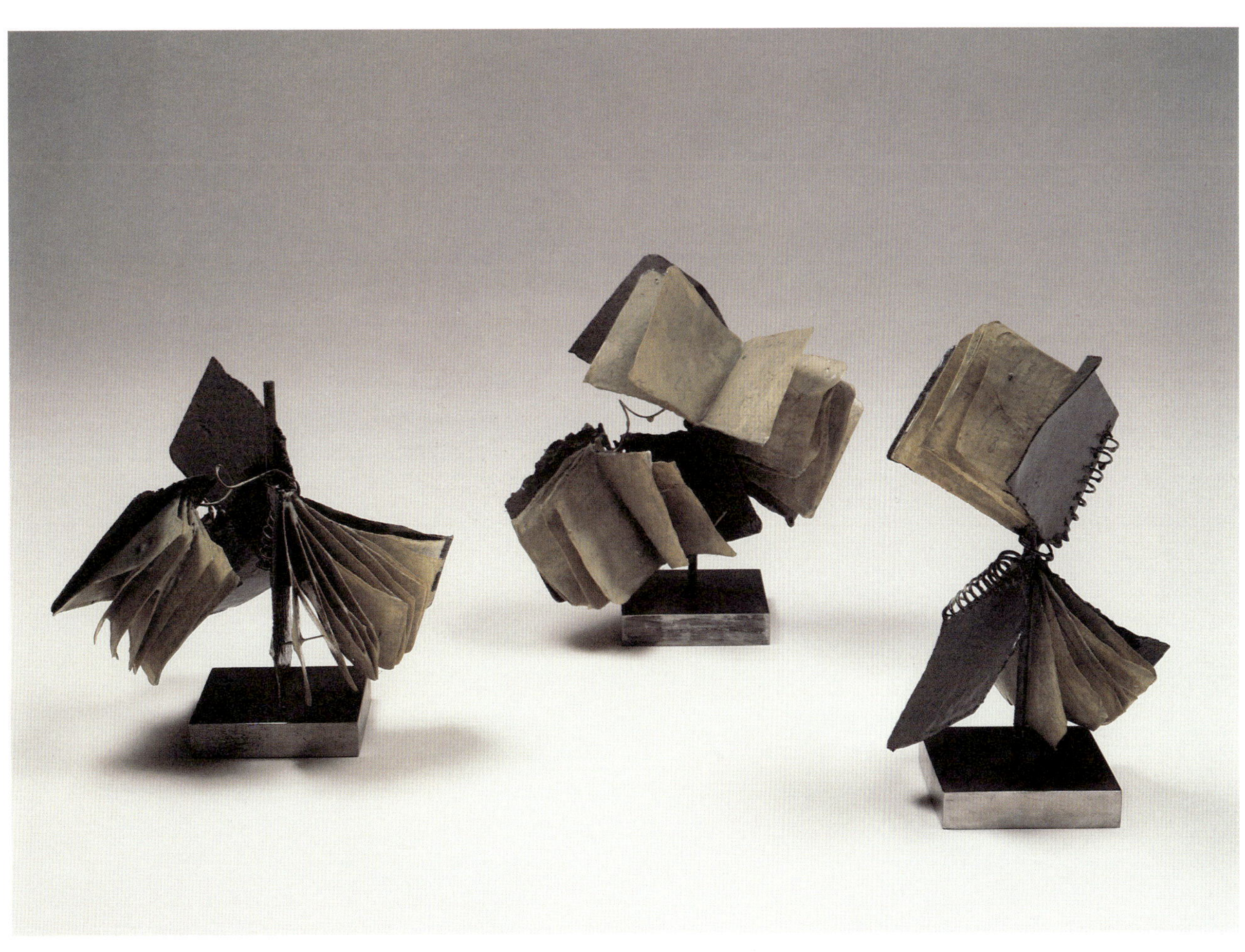

Torn Notebook Studies A, B, C, 1992
notebooks, resin and latex paint, mounted on steel bases
A: 8 x 5 1/4 x 4 1/4" B: 6 3/4 x 6 1/2 x 6 3/8" C: 7 1/8 x 7 1/2 x 4 3/4"

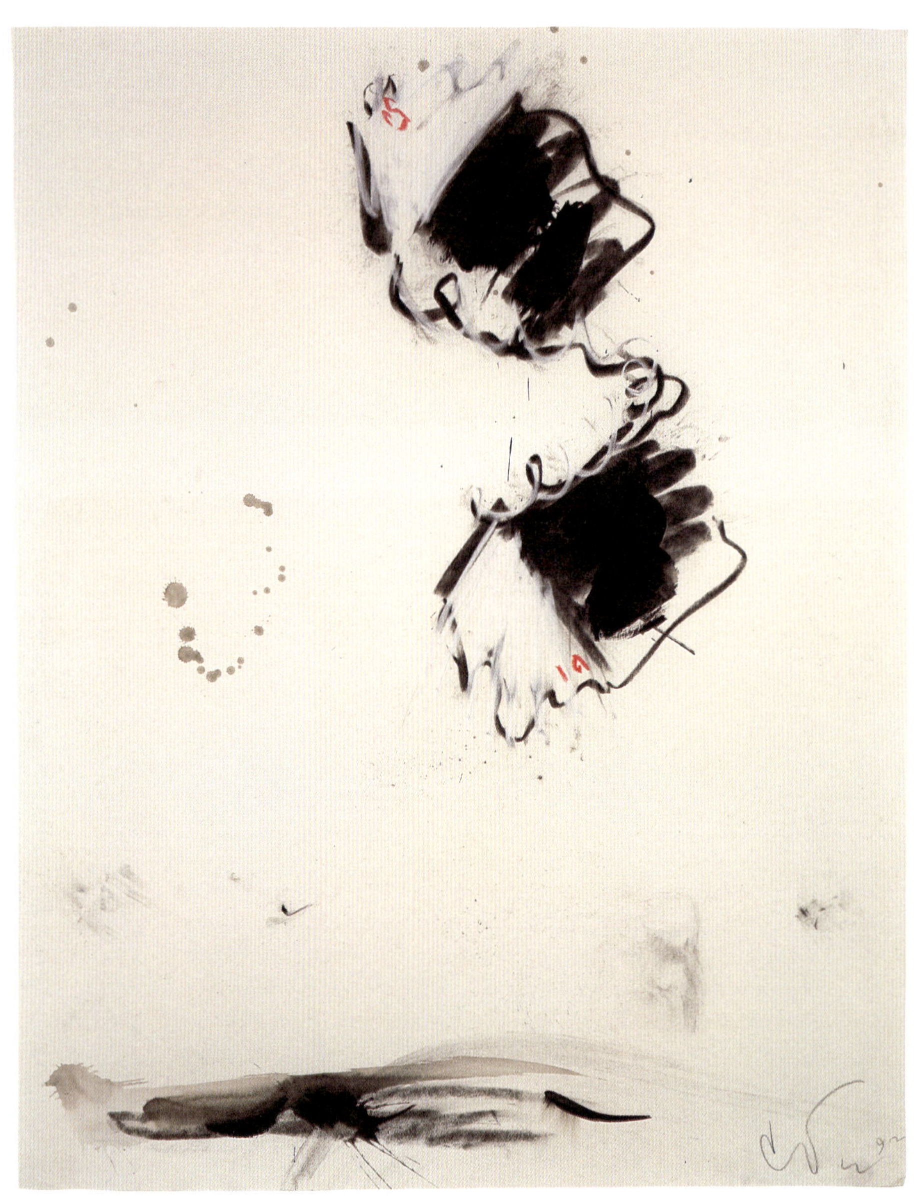

Torn Notebook, 1992
charcoal, pastel and watercolor
29 x 23"

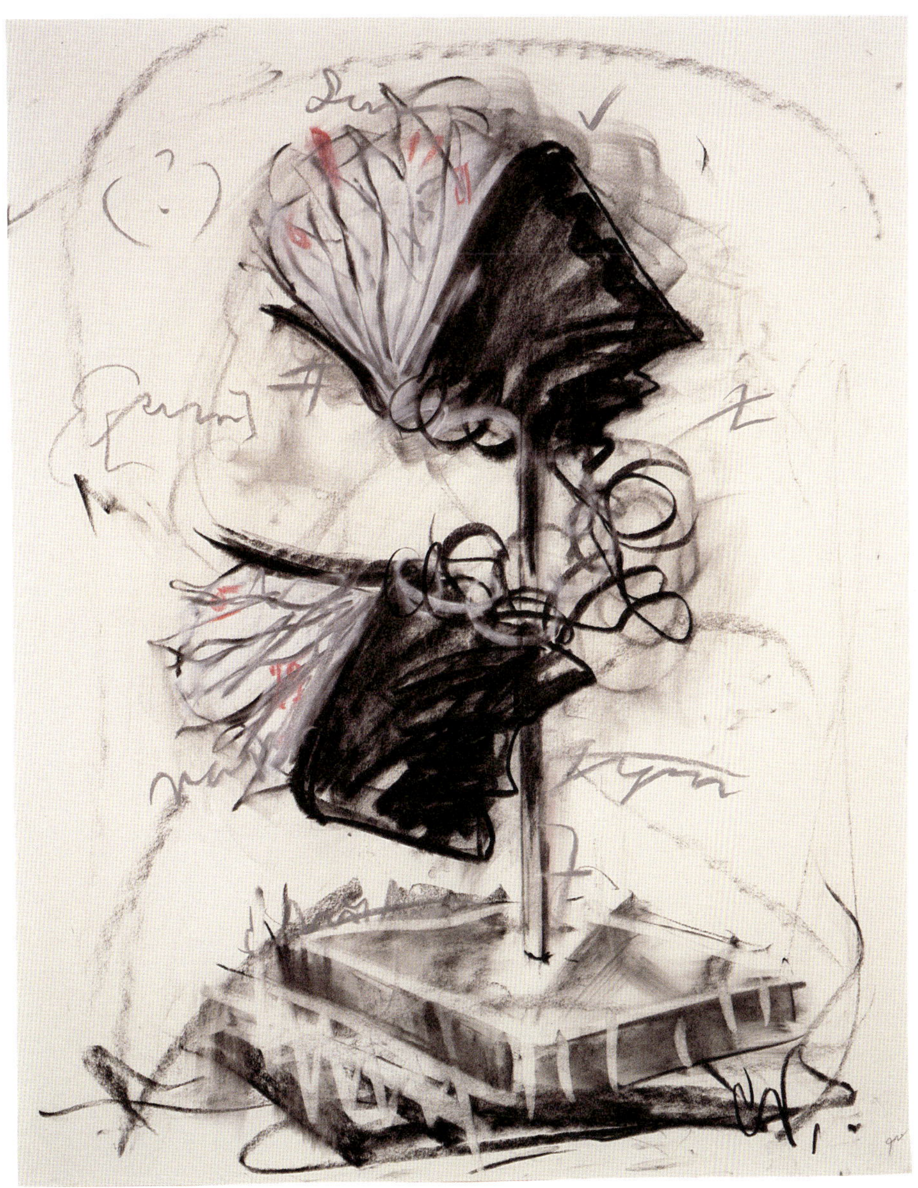

Study for a Sculpture of a Torn Notebook, 1992
charcoal and pastel
29 x 23"

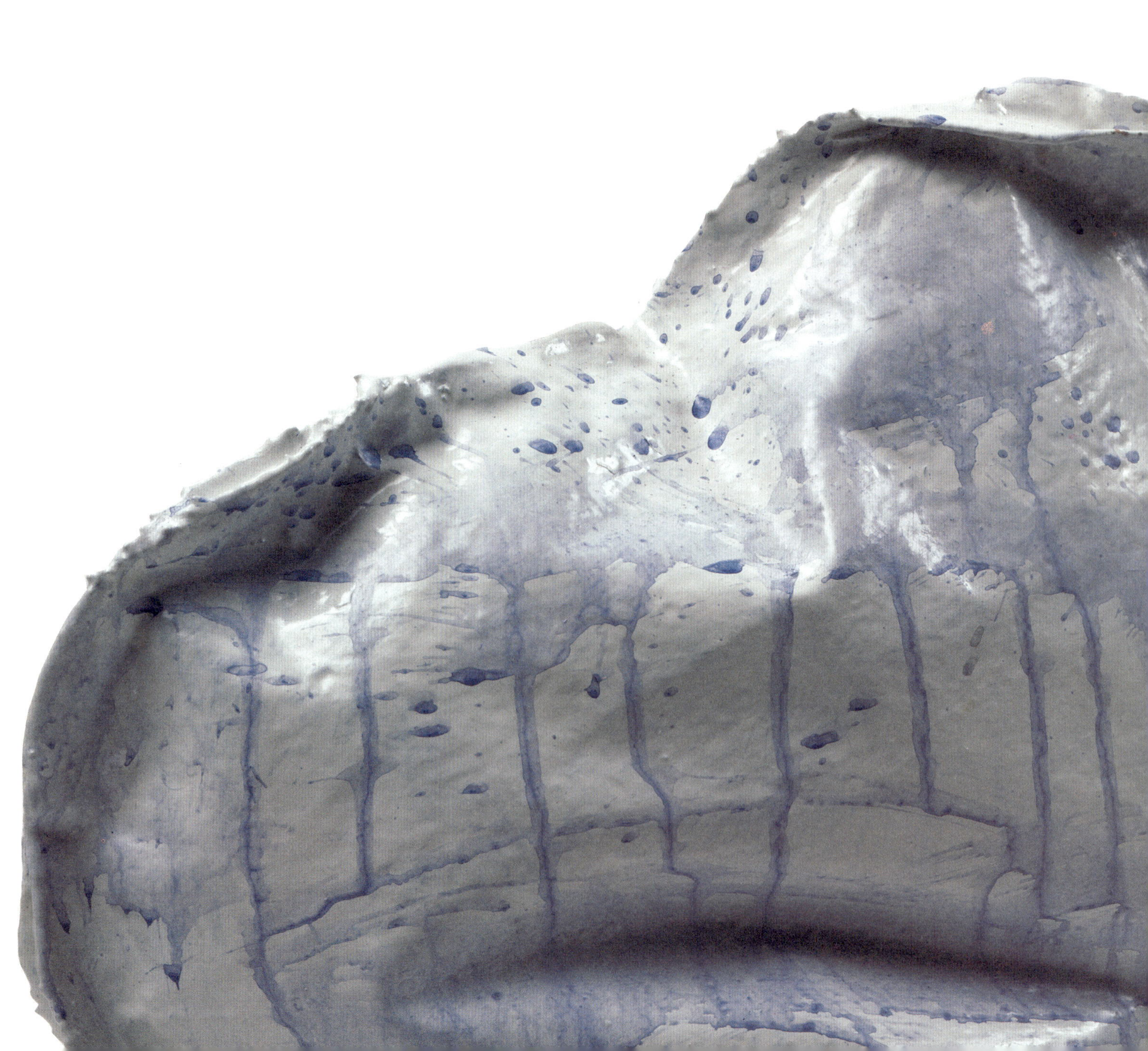

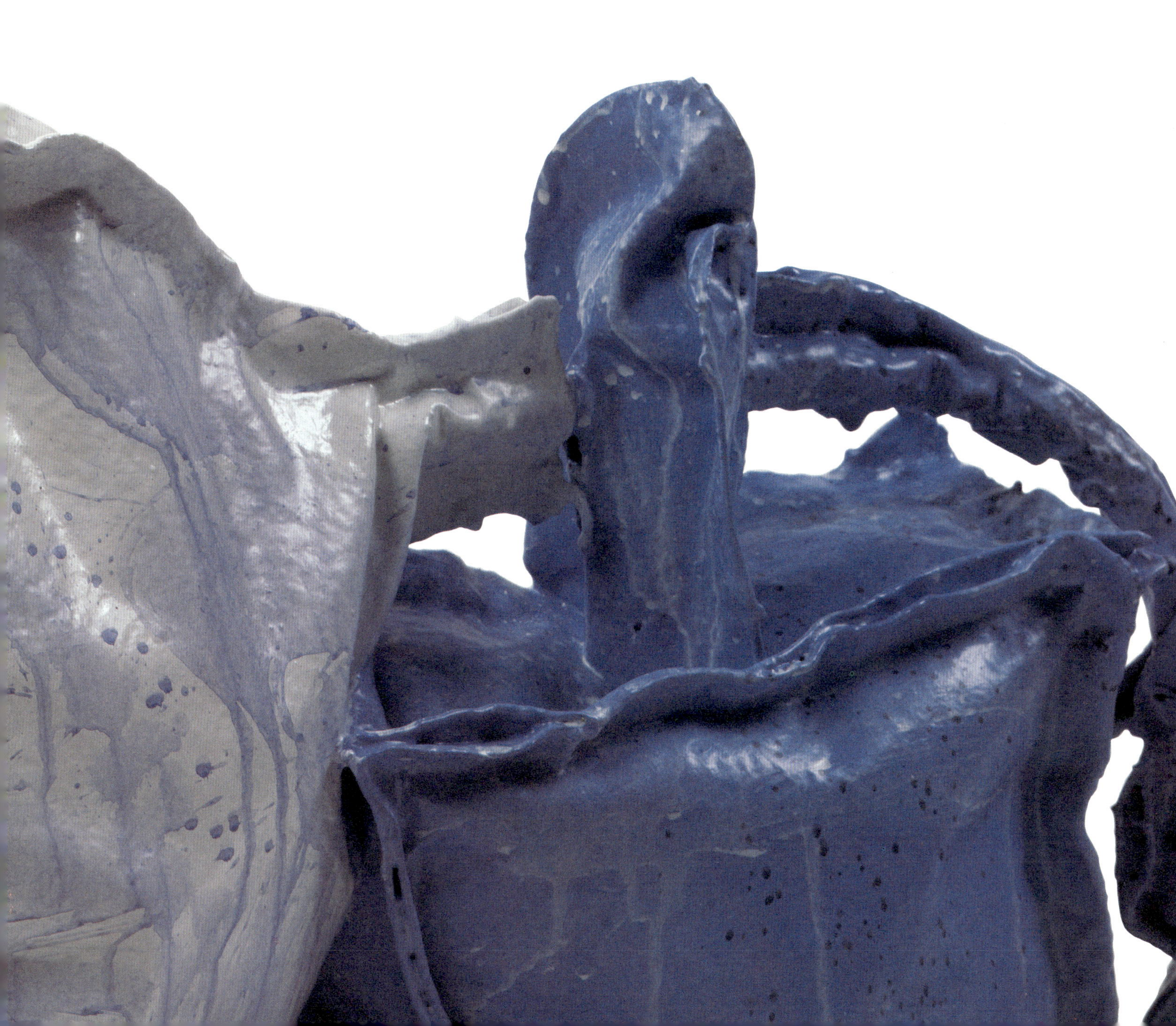

Perfume Bottle, Pink, 1992
muslin, wood, clothesline, dacron, resin and latex paint
14½ x 9¾ x 38½" attached to ½ x 8 x 30" painted aluminum base

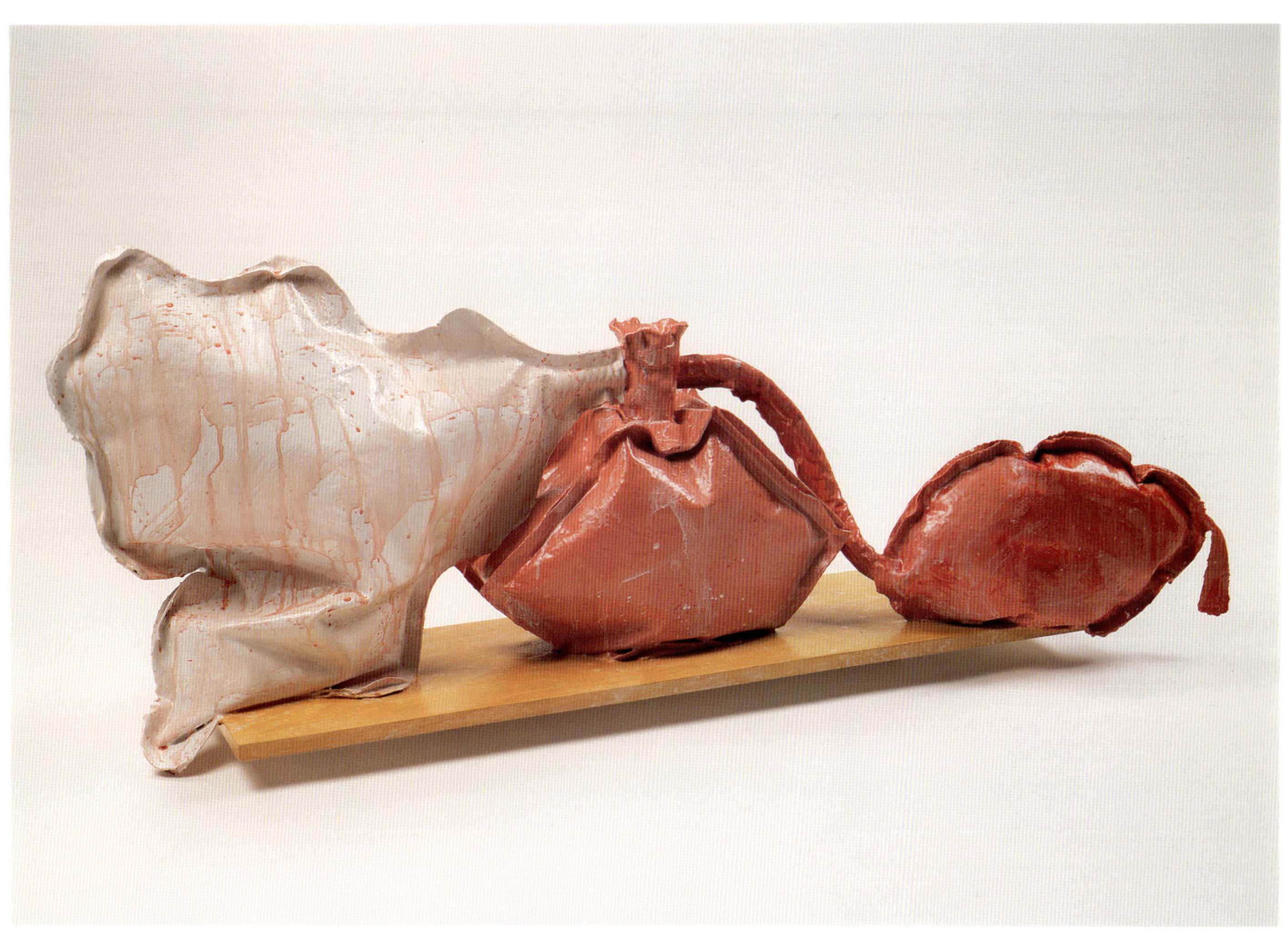

Perfume Bottle, Blue, 1992
muslin, wood, clothesline, dacron, resin and latex paint
12½ x 9¼ x 34¾" attached to ½ x 8 x 30" painted aluminum base

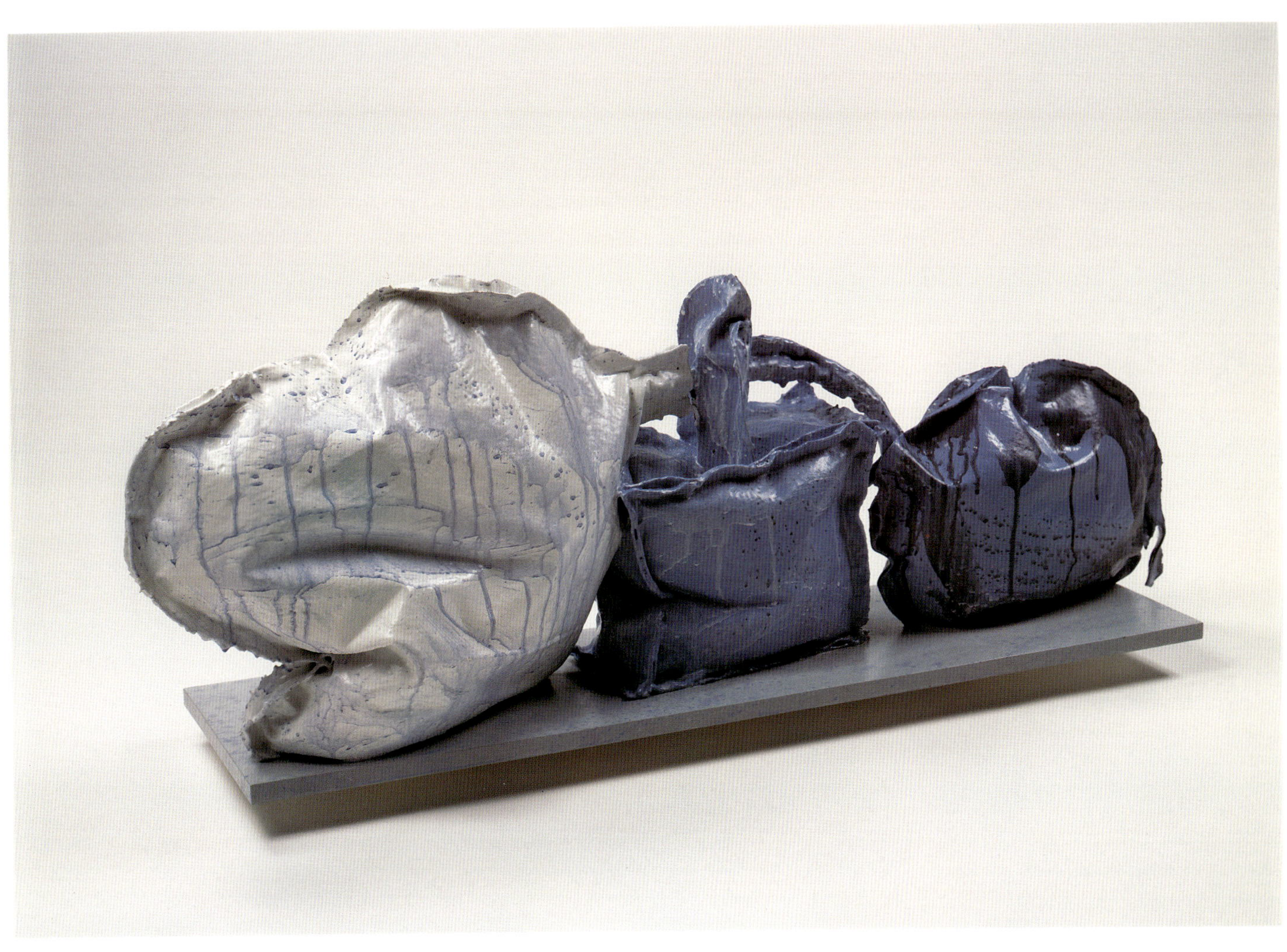

Perfume Bottle, Yellow, 1992
muslin, wood, clothesline, dacron, resin and latex paint
14 5/8 x 8 1/8 x 41 1/4" attached to 1/2 x 8 x 30" painted aluminum base

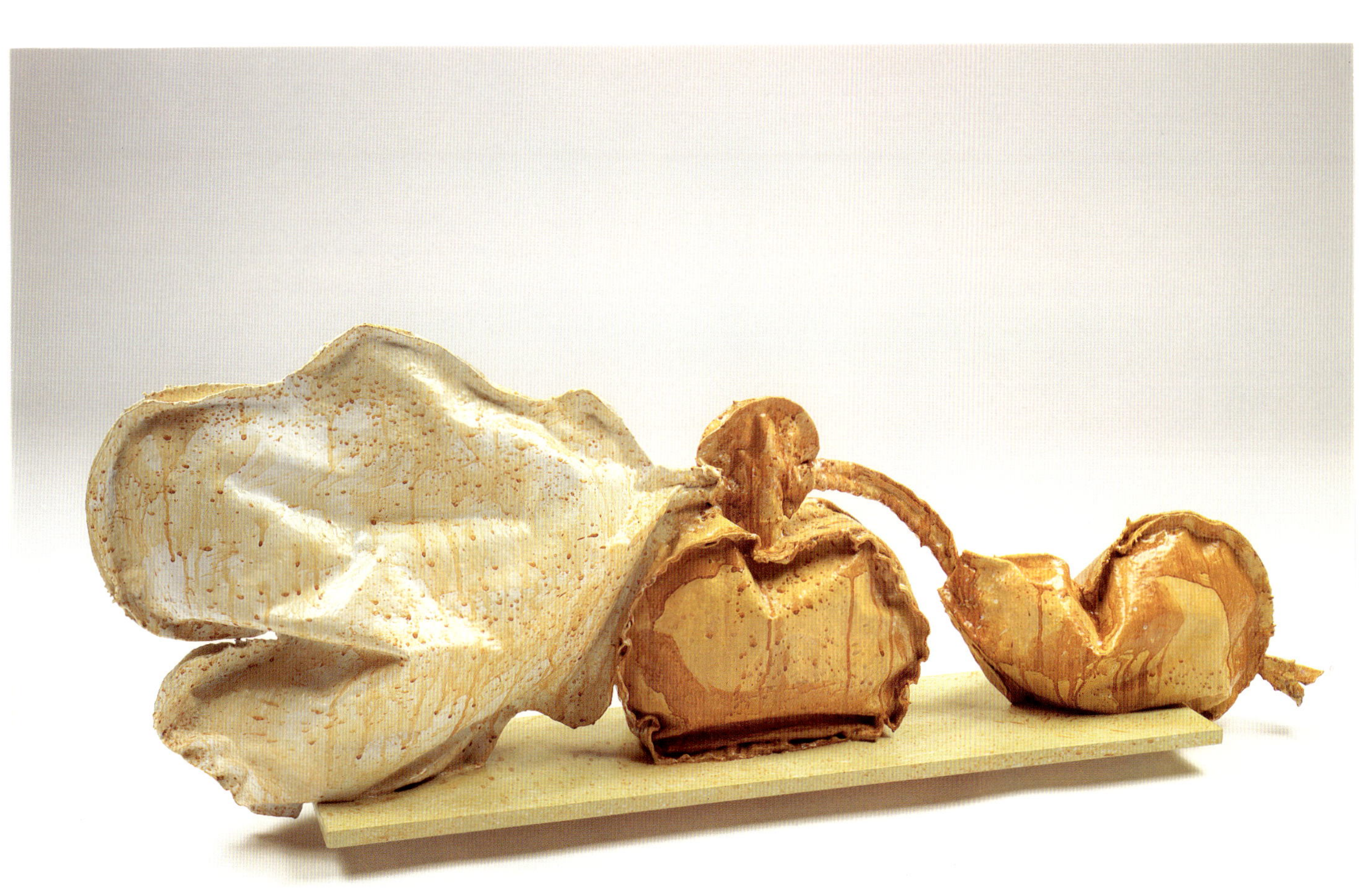

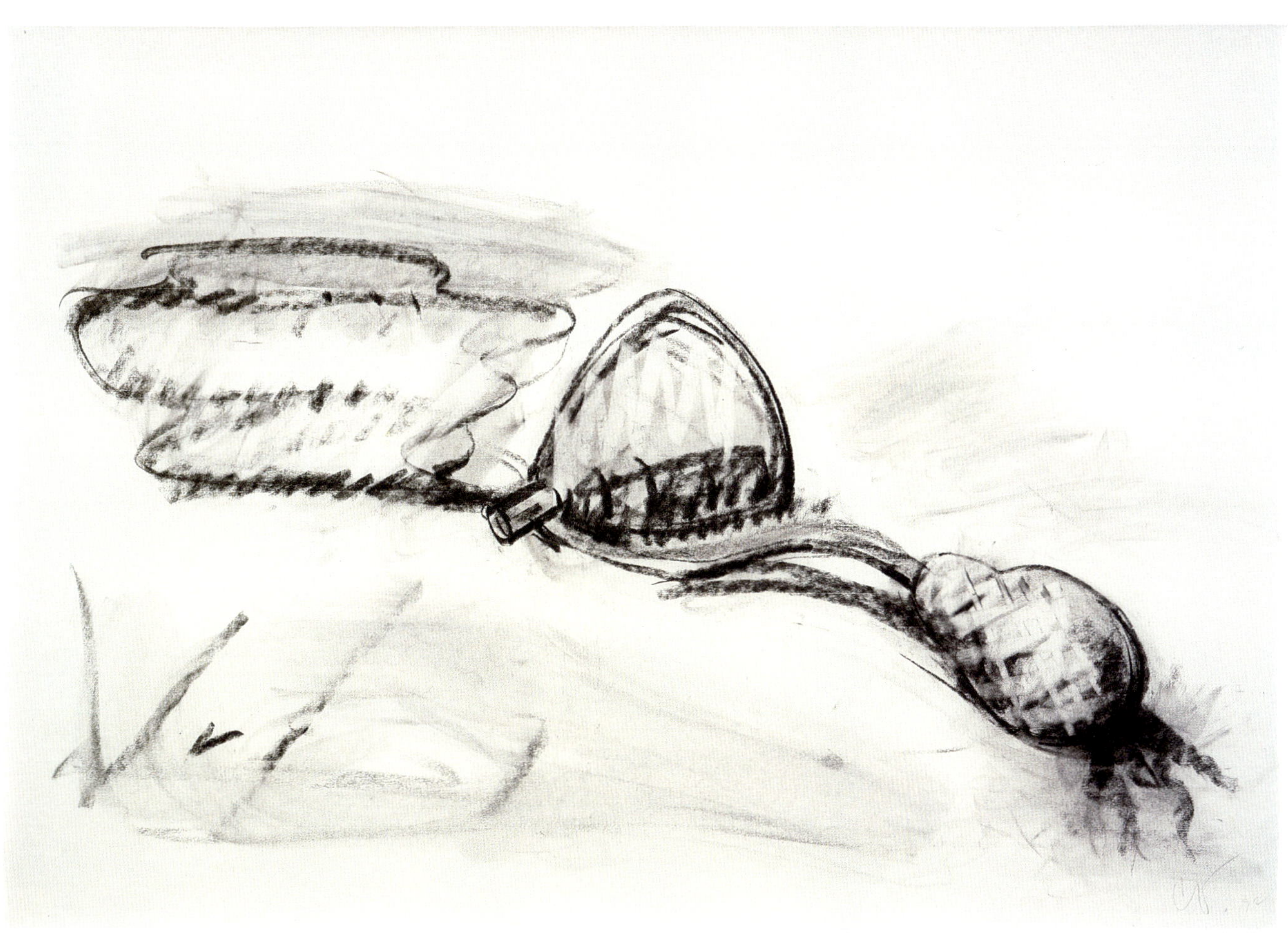

Perfume Bottle, Fallen, 1992
charcoal
25¾ x 37¾"

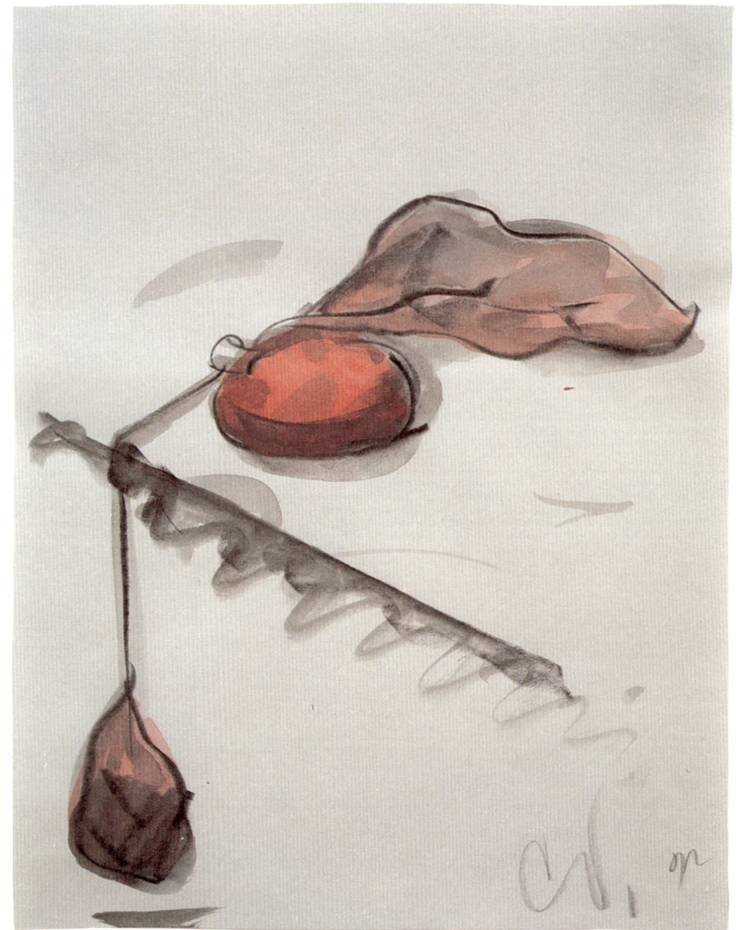

Perfume Bottle, Fallen, Atomizer Over Edge, 1992
crayon, pastel and watercolor
13¾ x 11"

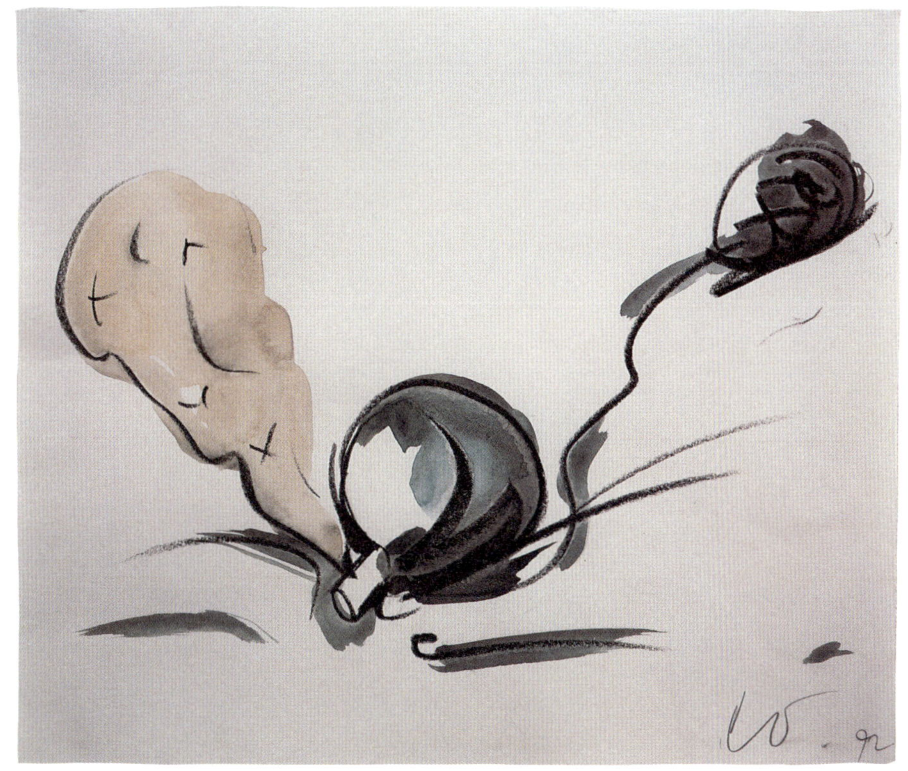

Perfume Bottle, Fallen, 1992
crayon and watercolor
13 x 15¾"

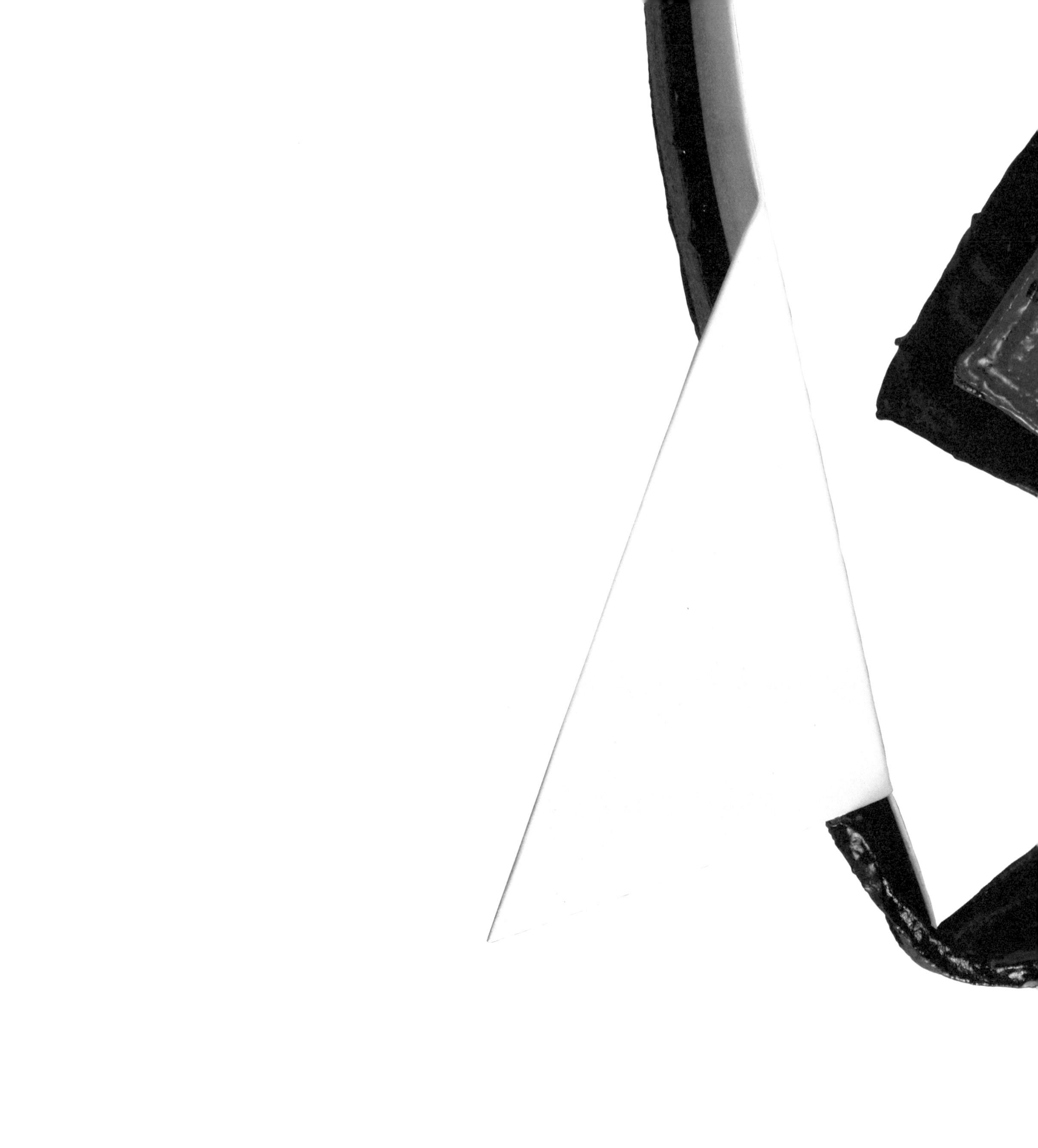

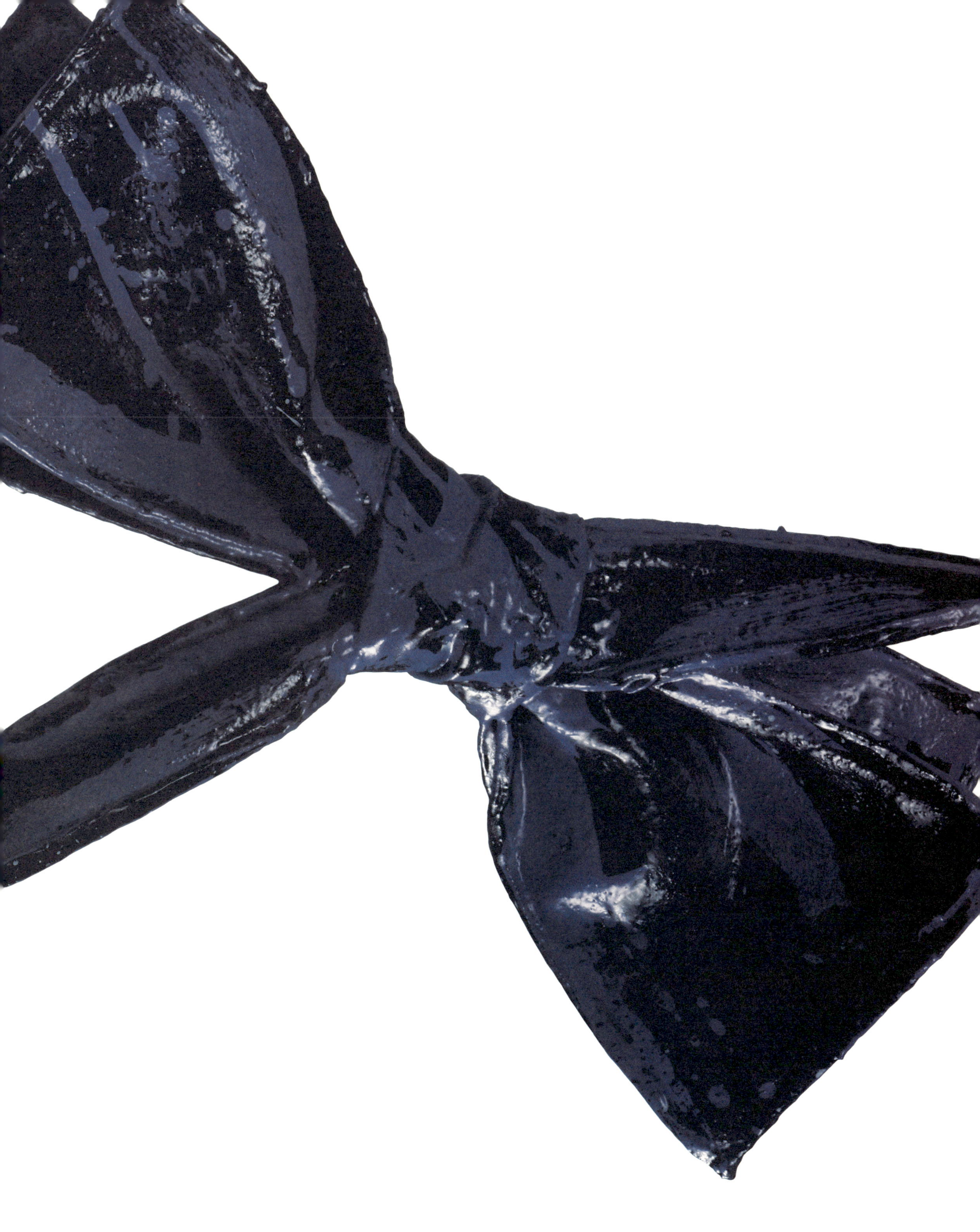

Standing Collar with Bow Tie, 1992
steel, canvas, ethafoam, resin and latex paint
34 3/4 x 9 1/2 x 40"

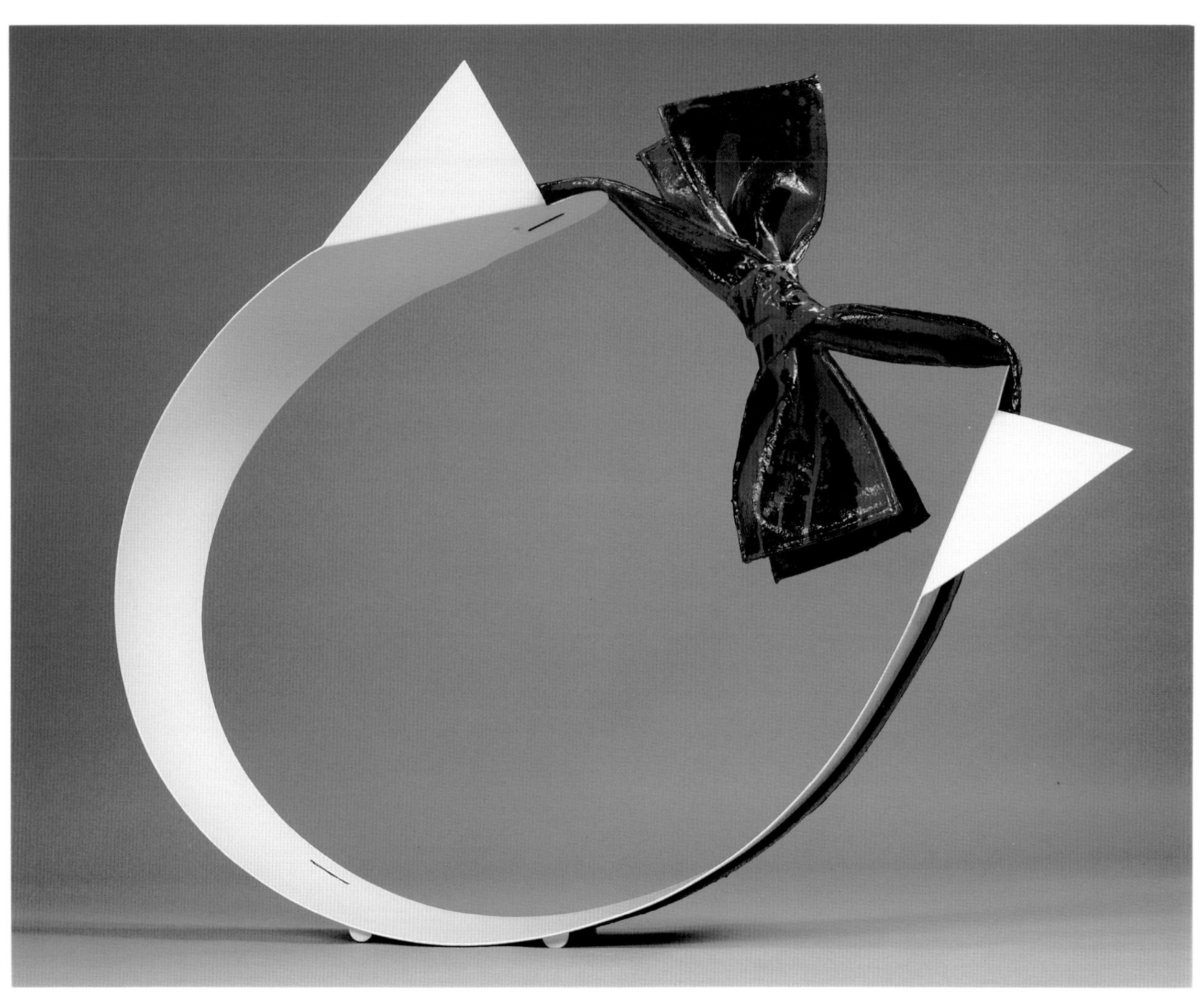

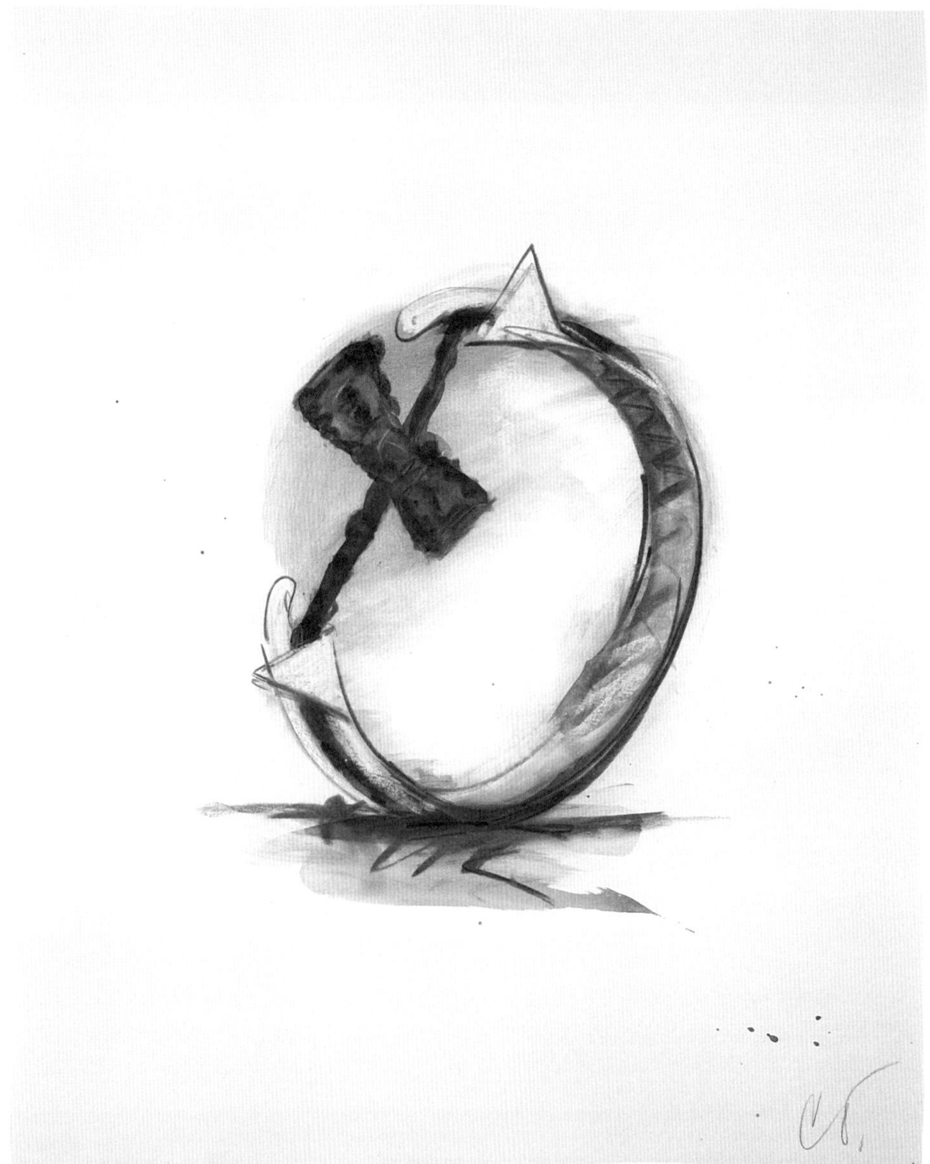

Standing Collar with Bow Tie, 1992
charcoal, pastel and watercolor
29½ x 24"

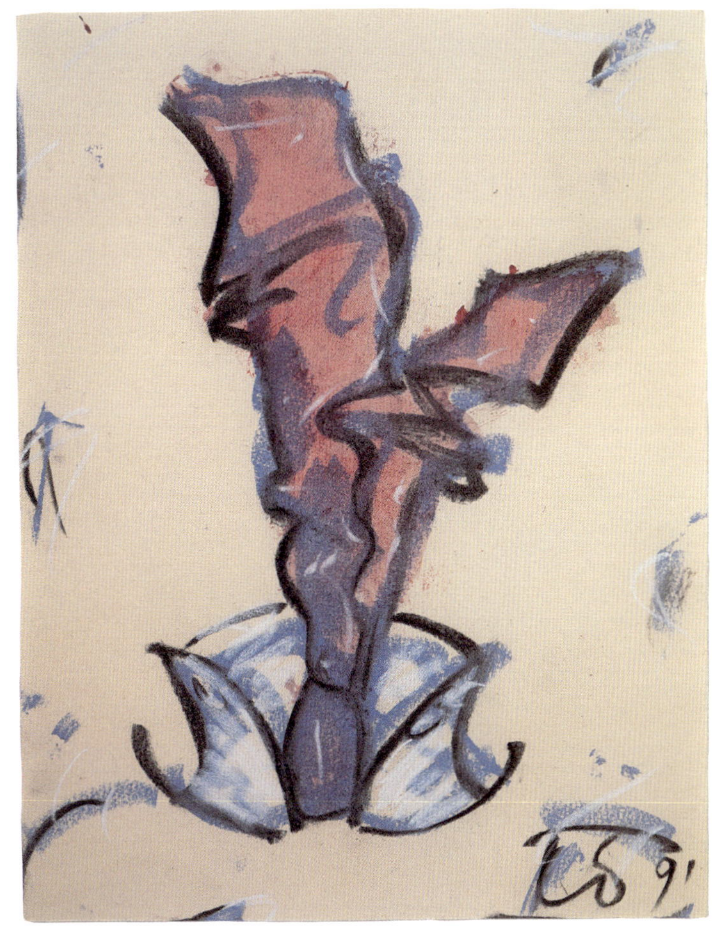

Inverted Tie and Collar, 1992
charcoal, pastel and watercolor
14 x 11"

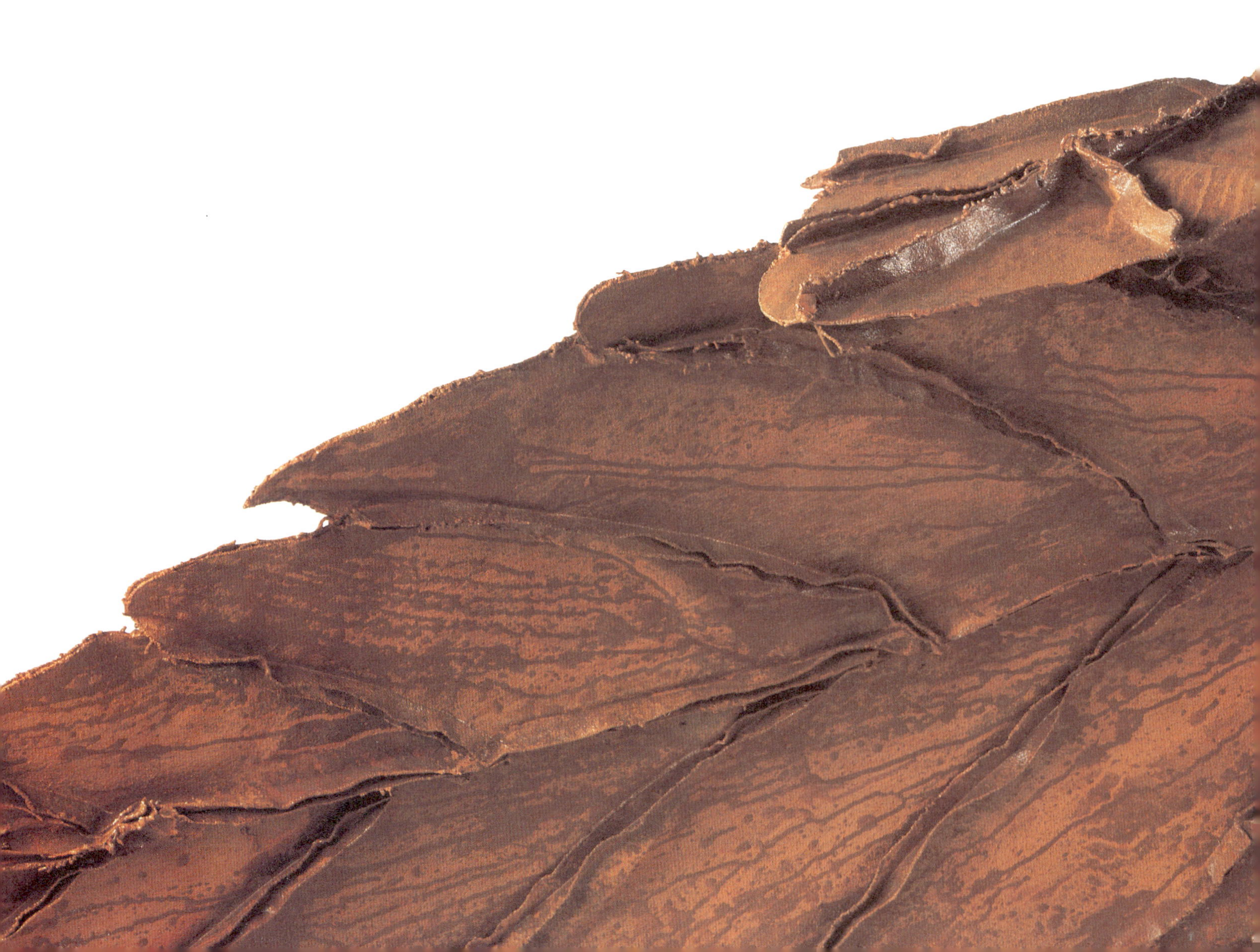

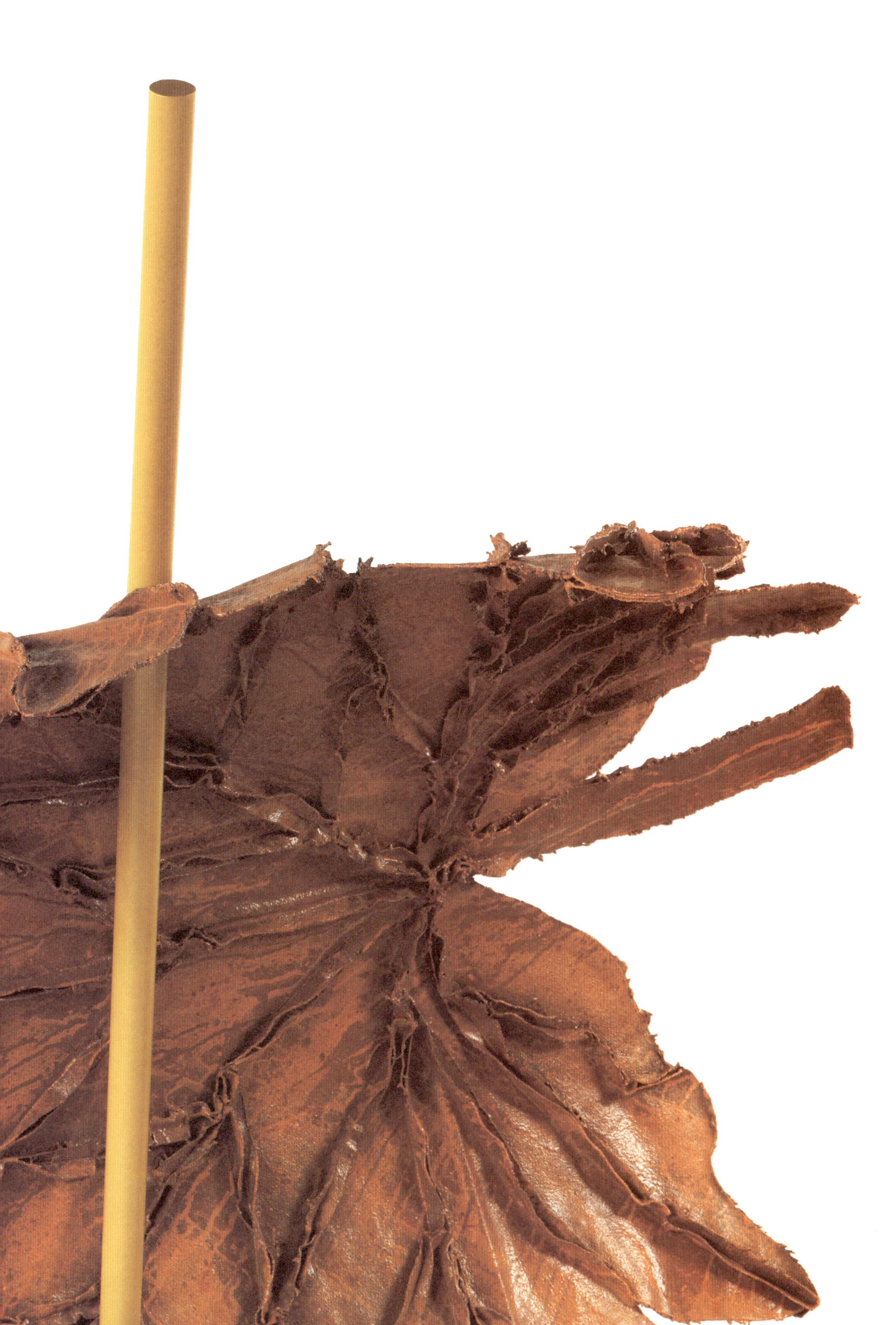

Leaf Boat, 1992
canvas, steel, aluminum, cardboard, resin and latex paint
Sail: 80 x 29 x 90¾"   Boat: 5⅜ x 49 x 76½"

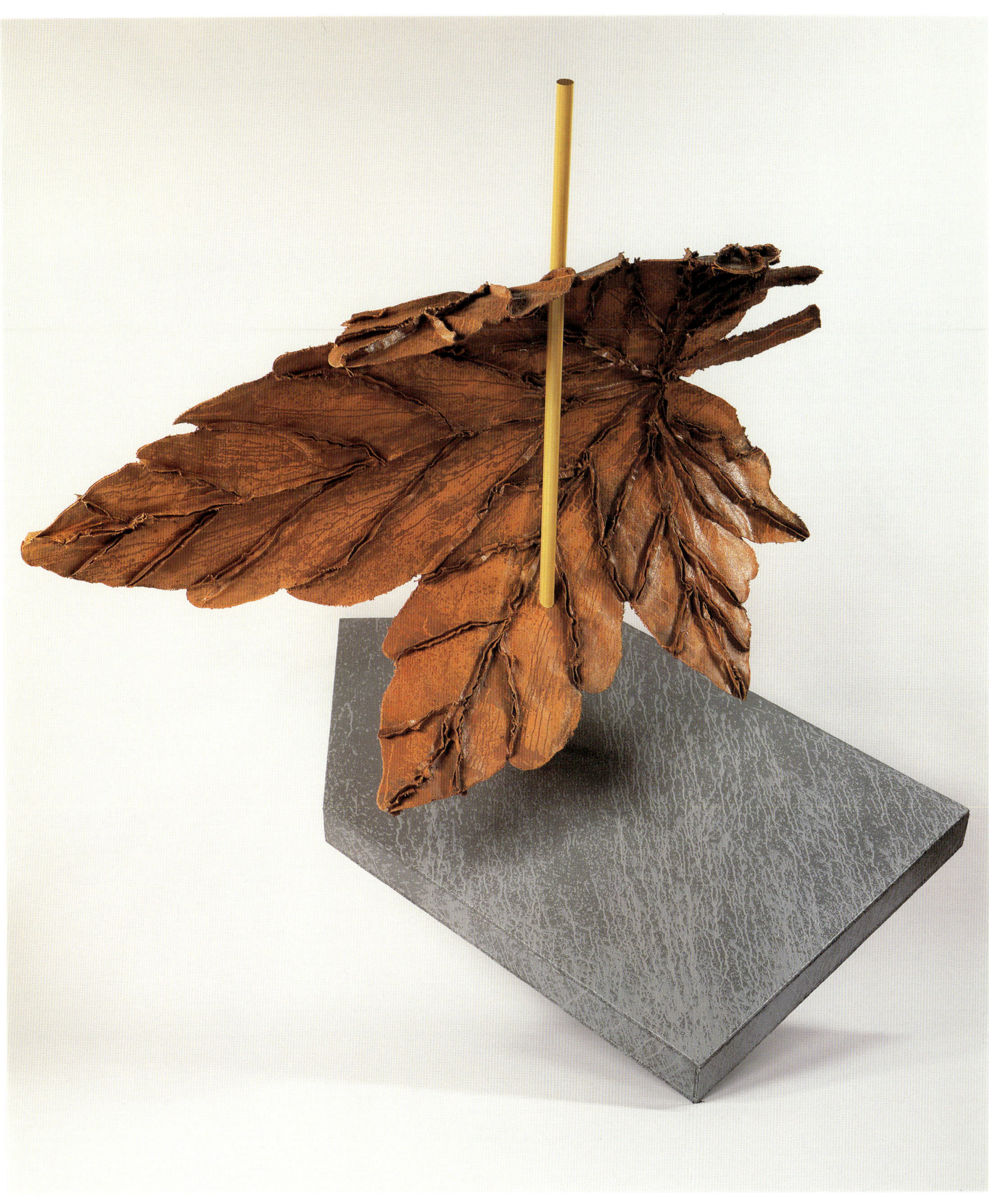

Floating Cargo, 1992, (Detail)
canvas, urethane foam, expanded polystyrene, cardboard, resin and latex paint
Apple Core: 12¾ x 28¾ x 65" *Ice Cream Stick*: 4¼ x 11 x 48½" *Peanut Shell*: 8¼ x 15½ x 35¾"
Potato Chip: 5¾ x 35½" diameter *Cork*: 14¾ x 10½ x 15½"

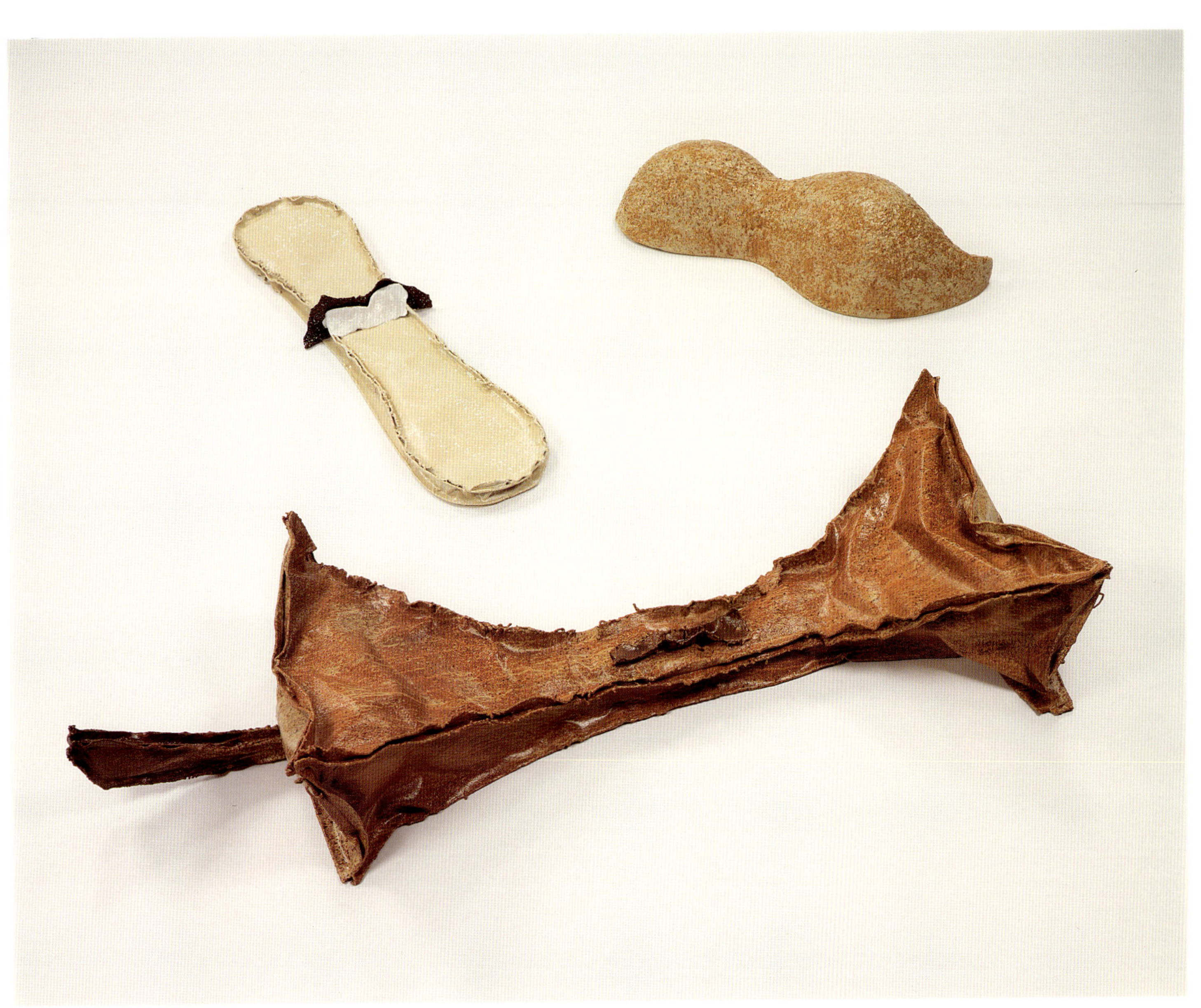

Leaf Boat with Floating Cargo, Model, 1992
canvas, wood, wire, cardboard, latex paint and five altered objects:
apple core, ice cream stick, peanut shell, potato chip and cork
11¾ x 11 x 11¾"

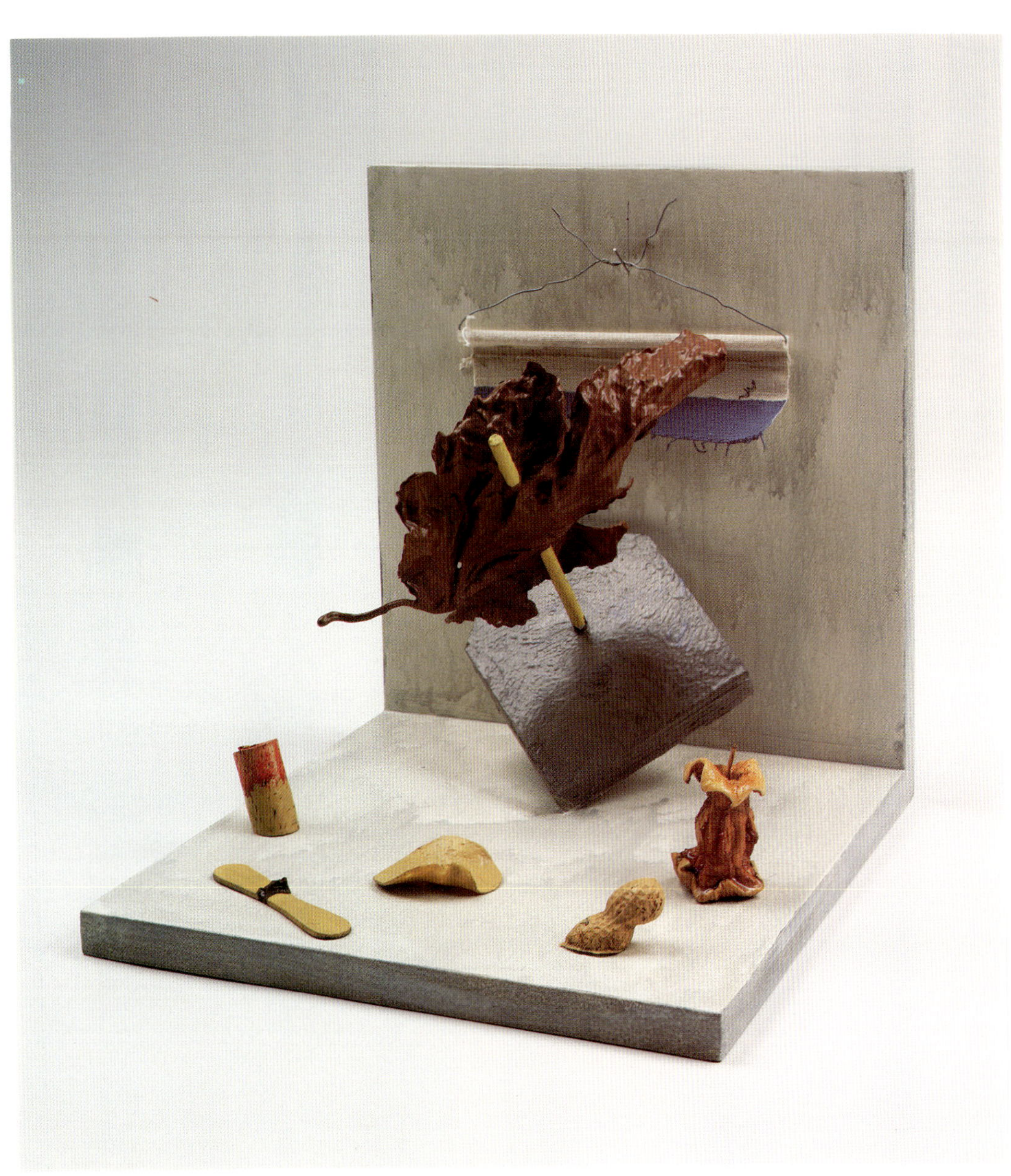

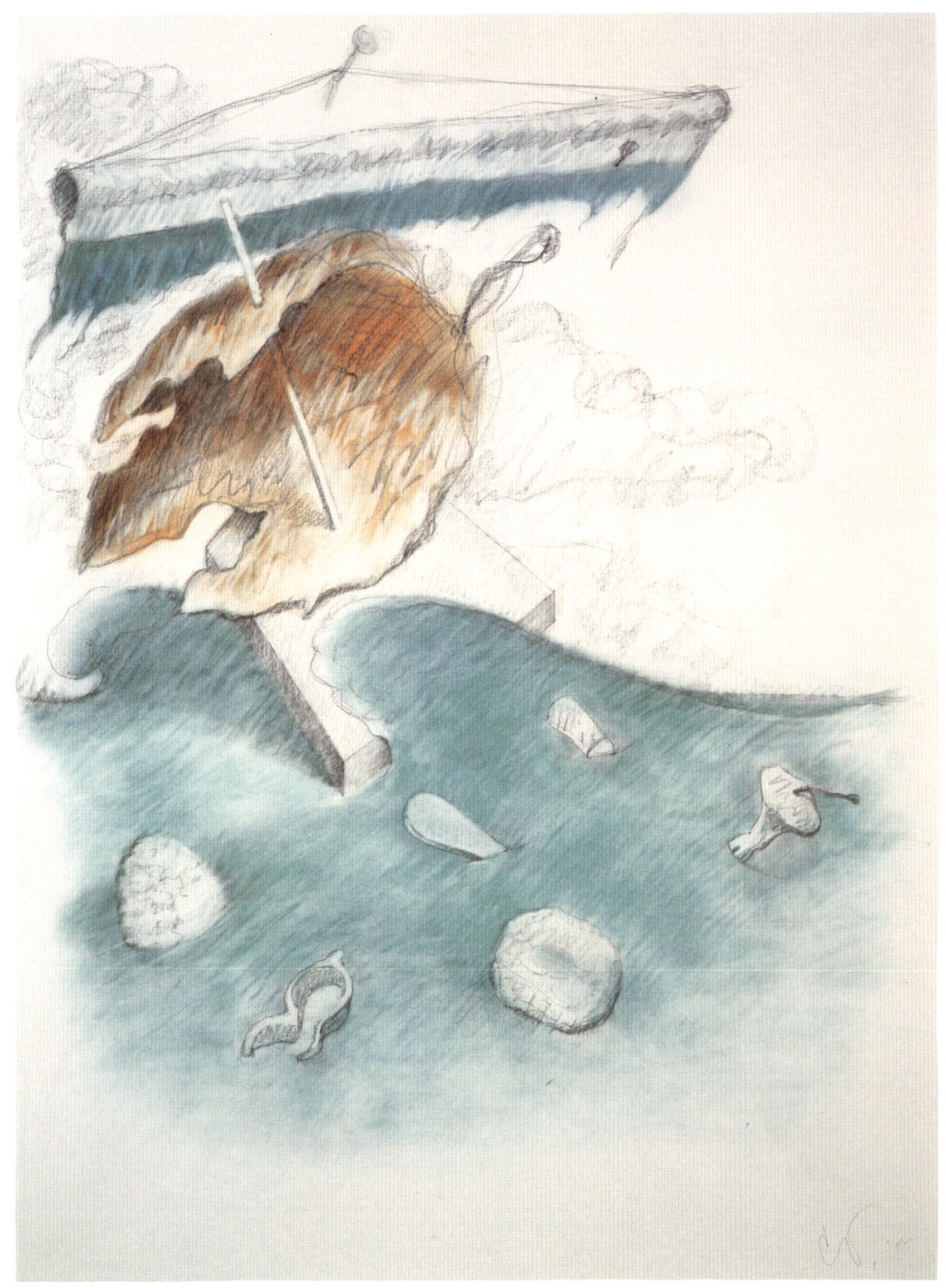

Leaf Boat Study, Storm in the Studio, 1992
pencil and pastel
40 x 30"

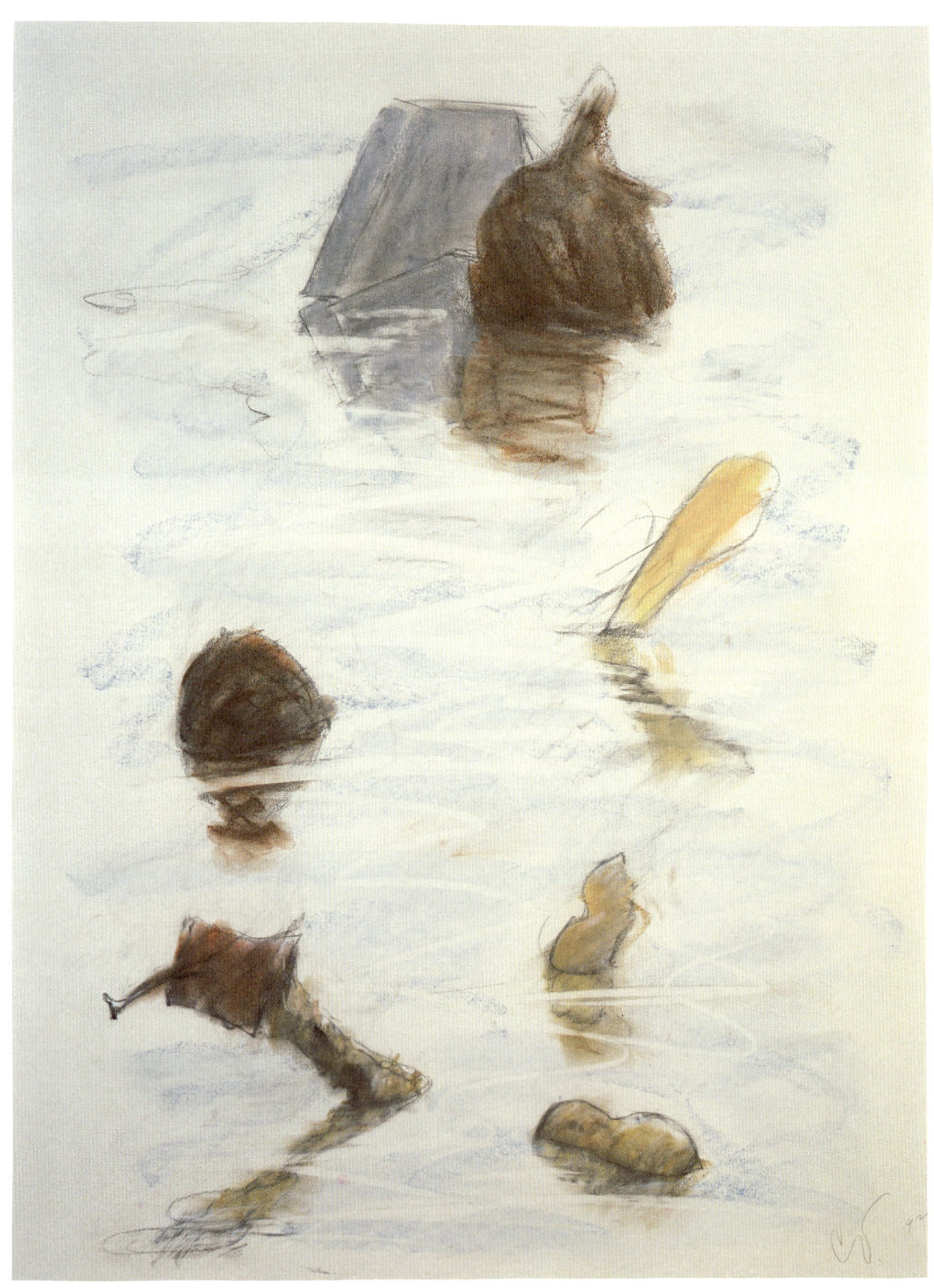

Capsized Leaf Boat, 1992
pencil and pastel
40 x 30"

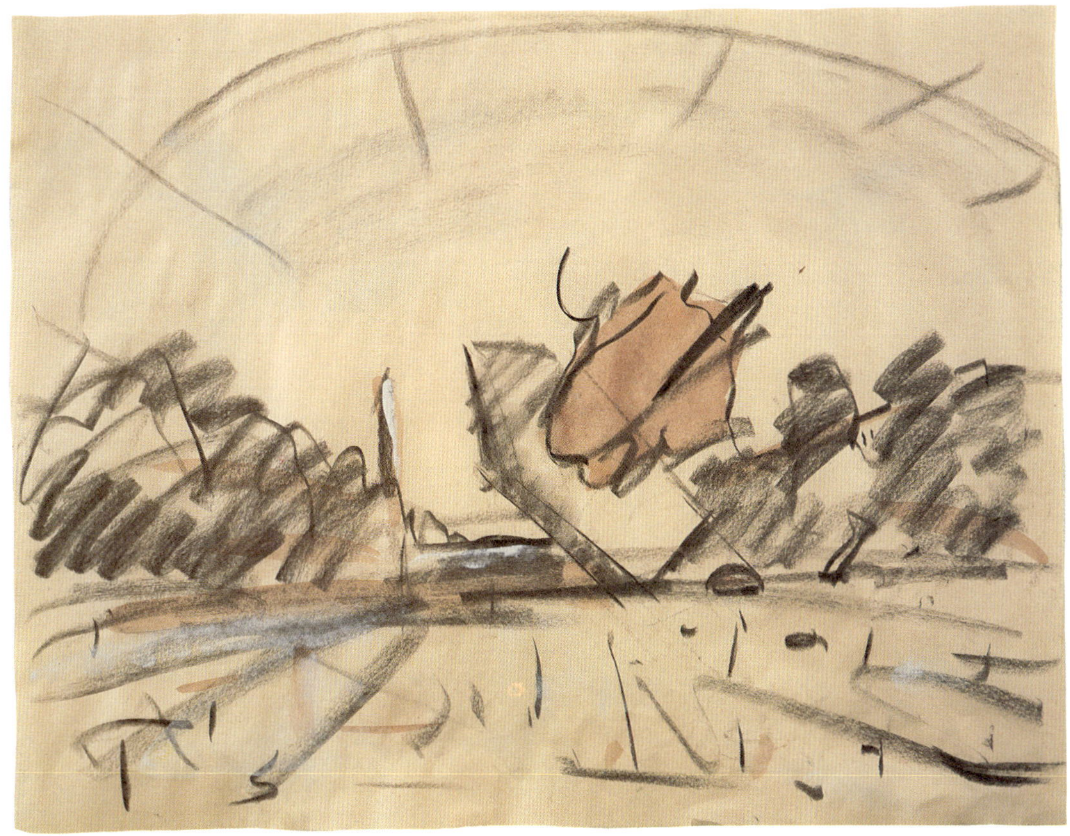

Study for a Sculpture in the Form of a Leaf Boat, Les Tuileries, Paris, 1992
charcoal and watercolor
18 x 24"

List of Works in Catalogue

Soft Saxophone, Scale A, 1992
muslin, wood, clothesline, dacron, resin and latex paint
32 x 12½ x 15"

Soft Saxophone, Scale A, Vinyl, 1992
vinyl, urethane foam and wood
38½" attached to ½ x 24 x 24" base

Soft Saxophone, Scale A, Muslin, 1992
muslin, hardware cloth, urethane foam, wood, dacron and latex paint
11¼ x 27 x 49"

Soft Saxophone, Scale B, 1992
canvas, wood, clothesline, dacron, resin and latex paint
69 x 35 x 36"

Soft Harp, Scale A, 1992
muslin, steel, clothesline, dacron, resin and latex paint
51½ x 27 x 7½"

Soft Harp, Scale A, Harp Sail, 1992
muslin, dacron, sash cord, wood, aluminum and latex paint
65½ x 8 x 27" attached to 1 x 12 x 27" aluminum and wood base

Soft Harp, Scale B, Ghost Harp, 1992
canvas, steel, aluminum, clothesline, expanded polystyrene, dacron and latex paint
95 x 27 x 48"

Soft Harp, Scale C, Harp Sail, 1992
wood, steel, aluminum, clothesline, feathers and latex paint
98 x 24 x 123½"

Clarinet Bridge, 1992
canvas, wood, clothesline, urethane foam, resin and latex paint
14½ x 11¼ x 98"

Saxophone Fountain, 1992
charcoal, crayon and watercolor
20 x 26"

Harps in Séance, 1992
pastel
14 x 17"

Soft Harp, Plan, 1992
pencil
40 x 30"

Torn Notebook, One, 1992
muslin, chicken wire, clothesline, steel, resin, and latex paint
24 x 25 x 19" attached to ½ x 24 x 24" aluminum plate

Torn Notebook, Two, 1992
muslin, chicken wire, clothesline, steel, resin and latex paint
30 x 24½ x 24" attached to ½ x 12 x 12" painted aluminum plate

Torn Notebook, Three, 1992
muslin, chicken wire, clothesline, steel, resin and latex paint
24 x 33 x 36" attached to ½ x 8¼ x 8¼" aluminum plate

Torn Notebook Studies A, B, C, 1992
notebooks, resin and latex paint, mounted on steel bases
A: 8 x 5¼ x 4¼" B: 6¾ x 6½ x 6⅜" C: 7⅛ x 7½ x 4¾"

Torn Notebook, 1992
charcoal, pastel and watercolor
29 x 23"

Study for a Sculpture of a Torn Notebook, 1992
charcoal and pastel
29 x 23"

Perfume Bottle, Pink, 1992
muslin, wood, clothesline, dacron, resin and latex paint
14½ x 9¾ x 38½" attached to ½ x 8 x 30" painted aluminum base

Perfume Bottle, Blue, 1992
muslin, wood, clothesline, dacron, resin and latex paint
12½ x 9¼ x 34¾" attached to ½ x 8 x 30" painted aluminum base

Perfume Bottle, Yellow, 1992
muslin, wood, clothesline, dacron, resin and latex paint
14⅝ x 8⅛ x 41¼" attached to ½ x 8 x 30" painted aluminum base

Perfume Bottle, Fallen, 1992
charcoal
25¾ x 37¾"

Perfume Bottle, Fallen, Atomizer Over Edge, 1992
crayon, pastel and watercolor
13¾ x 11"

Perfume Bottle, Fallen, 1992
crayon and watercolor
13 x 15¾"

Standing Collar with Bow Tie, 1992
steel, canvas, ethafoam, resin and latex paint
34¾ x 9½ x 40"

Standing Collar with Bow Tie, 1992
charcoal, pastel and watercolor
29½ x 24"

Inverted Tie and Collar, 1992
charcoal, pastel and watercolor
14 x 11"

Leaf Boat, 1992
canvas, steel, aluminum, cardboard, resin and latex paint
Sail: 80 x 29 x 90¾" Boat: 5⅜ x 49 x 76½"

Floating Cargo, 1992 (detail)
canvas, urethane foam, expanded polystyrene, cardboard, resin and latex paint
Apple Core: 12¾ x 28¾ x 65" *Ice Cream Stick*: 4¼ x 11 x 48½" *Peanut Shell*: 8¼ x 15½ x 35¾"
Potato Chip: 5¾ x 35½" diameter *Cork*: 14¾ x 10½ x 15½"

Leaf Boat with Floating Cargo, Model, 1992
canvas, wood, wire, cardboard, latex paint and five altered objects:
apple core, ice cream stick, peanut shell, potato chip and cork
11¾ x 11 x 11¾"

Leaf Boat Study, Storm in the Studio, 1992
pencil and pastel
40 x 30"

Capsized Leaf Boat, 1992
pencil and pastel
40 x 30"

Study for a Sculpture in the Form of a Leaf Boat, Les Tuileries, Paris, 1992
charcoal and watercolor
18 x 24"

Biography

Claes Oldenburg was born in Stockholm, Sweden on January 28, 1929. After living in New York City; Rye, New York; and Oslo, Norway, his family settled in Chicago in 1936. Oldenburg attended Yale University 1946-50, and then returned to Chicago where he worked as an apprentice reporter at the City News Bureau and studied at the Art Institute of Chicago. He became an American citizen in December 1953. In 1956 he moved to New York City, where he has lived since, except for travels to Europe and Japan and a year-and-a-half in Deventer, The Netherlands. Oldenburg is married to Coosje van Bruggen, with whom he has worked on large-scale public projects and performances since 1976.

Selected Solo Exhibitions

1959
Judson Gallery, Judson Memorial Church, New York.
Drawings Sculptures Poems by Claes Oldenburg.

1960
Reuben Gallery, New York. *The Street.*

1961
107 East 2nd Street, New York. *The Store.*

1962
Green Gallery, New York.

1963
Dwan Gallery, Los Angeles.

1964
Sidney Janis Gallery, New York.

The Pace Gallery, Boston.

Galerie Ileana Sonnabend, Paris.

1966
Sidney Janis Gallery, New York.

Robert Fraser Gallery, London.

Moderna Museet, Stockholm.

1967
Sidney Janis Gallery, New York.

Museum of Contemporary Art, Chicago. *Projects for Monuments.*

1968
Irving Blum Gallery, Los Angeles.

1969
Richard Feigen Gallery, Chicago. *Chicago Show.*

The Museum of Modern Art, New York. Traveled to Stedelijk Museum, Amsterdam; Städtische Kunsthalle, Düsseldorf; Tate Gallery, London.

1970
Sidney Janis Gallery, New York.

Margo Leavin Gallery, Los Angeles. *Works In Edition.*

1971
Pasadena Art Museum, Pasadena, California. *Object Into Monument.* Traveled to University Art Museum, University of California at Berkeley, Berkeley; The Nelson-Atkins Museum, Kansas City, Missouri; Des Moines Art Center, Des Moines, Iowa; Philadelphia Museum of Art, Philadelphia; The Art Institute of Chicago, Chicago.

1973
M. Knoedler & Co., New York. *Recent Prints.*

Minami Gallery, Tokyo.

1974
The New Gallery, Cleveland, Ohio; The Dayton Art Institute, Dayton, Ohio. *Standing Mitt with Ball.*

Leo Castelli Gallery, New York.

Yale University Art Gallery, Yale University, New Haven, Connecticut. *The Lipstick Comes Back.*

1975
Kunsthalle Tübingen, Tübingen, Germany. *Zeichnungen von Claes Oldenburg.* Traveled to Kunstmuseum Basel, Basel; Städtische Galerie im Lenbachhaus, Munich; Nationalgalerie, Berlin; Staatliche Museen Preußischer Kulturbesitz, Berlin; Kaiser Wilhelm Museum, Krefeld, Germany; Museum des 20. Jahrhunderts, Vienna; Kunstverein Hamburg, Hamburg, Germany; Städelsches Kunstinstitut und Städtische Galerie, Frankfurt; Kestner-Gesellschaft, Hannover, Germany; Louisiana Museum of Modern Art, Humlebaek, Denmark.

Walker Art Center, Minneapolis. *Oldenburg: Six Themes.* Traveled to Denver Art Museum, Denver; The Seattle Art Museum, Seattle; Institute of Contemporary Art and Hayden Gallery, Massachusetts Institute of Technology, Boston; The Art Gallery of Ontario, Toronto.

Mayor Gallery, London. *Erotic Fantasy Drawings.*

Margo Leavin Gallery, Los Angeles. *The Alphabet in L.A.*

1976
Leo Castelli Gallery, New York.

1977
Stedelijk Museum, Amsterdam. *Drawings, Watercolors and Graphics.* Traveled to Musée national d'art moderne, Centre Georges Pompidou, Paris; Moderna Museet, Stockholm.

Richard Gray Gallery, Chicago.

The Akron Art Institute, Akron, Ohio. *The Inverted Q.*

Museum of Contemporary Art, Chicago. *The Mouse Museum / The Ray Gun Wing: Two Collections / Two Buildings by Claes Oldenburg.* Traveled to Phoenix Art Museum, Phoenix, Arizona; St. Louis Art Museum, St. Louis, Missouri; Museum of Fine Arts, Dallas; Whitney Museum of American Art, New York; Rijksmuseum Kröller-Müller, Otterlo, The Netherlands; Museum Ludwig, Cologne.

1978
Margo Leavin Gallery, Los Angeles. *Sculptures, 1971-1977.*

1980
Leo Castelli Gallery, New York. *Large-Scale Projects 1977-1980.*

1985
Galerie Schmela, Düsseldorf. *Tube Supported by its Contents.*

1986
Palacio de Cristal, Parque del Retiro, Madrid. *El Cuchillo Barco.*

Leo Castelli Gallery, New York. *Props, Costumes and Designs from the Performance* Il Corso del Coltello *by Claes Oldenburg, Coosje van Bruggen, Frank O. Gehry.*

Solomon R. Guggenheim Museum, New York. *The Knife Ship.*

1987
Northern Centre for Contemporary Art, Sunderland, England. *A Bottle of Notes and Some Voyages.* Traveled to The Henry Moore Centre for the Study of Sculpture, Leeds City Art Gallery, Leeds, England; The Serpentine Gallery, London; The Glynn Vivian Art Gallery and Museum, Swansea, England; Palais des Beaux-Arts, Brussels; Wilhelm-Lehmbruck-Museum, Duisburg, Germany; IVAM Centre Julio González, Valencia, Spain; Tampereen Nykytaiteen Museo, Tampere, Finland.

Museum Haus Lange, Krefelder Kunstmuseen, Krefeld, Germany. *The Haunted House.*

Musée national d'art moderne, Centre Georges Pompidou, Paris. *Le couteau navire: décors, costumes, dessins:* Il Corso del Coltello, *de Claes Oldenburg, Coosje van Bruggen et Frank O. Gehry.*

Galerie Konrad Fischer, Düsseldorf. *Piano / Hammock.*

1988
Museum of Contemporary Art, Los Angeles. *The Knife Ship.*

Margo Leavin Gallery, Los Angeles. *Props, Costumes and Designs from the Performance* Il Corso del Coltello *by Claes Oldenburg, Coosje van Bruggen, Frank O. Gehry.*

Palais des Beaux-Arts, Brussels. *Drawings 1959-1988.* Traveled to Musée d'Art Contemporain, Nimes, France; IVAM Centre Julio González, Valencia, Spain.

1989
Musée d'Art Moderne, Saint-Etienne, France. *From the Entropic Library.*

1990
Carl Solway Gallery, Cincinnati, Ohio. *A Complete Survey of Sculptures in Edition 1963-1990.*

Galleria Christian Stein, Milan. *The European Desk Top.*

Brooke Alexander Editions, New York. *Multiples in Retrospect, 1964-1990.*

Leo Castelli Gallery, New York. (with Coosje van Bruggen)

Castelli Graphics, New York. *Lithographs from Gemini G.E.L. 1988-1990.*

The Mayor Gallery, London. *8 Sculptures 1961-1987.*

1991
Seagram Plaza, New York. *Monument to the Last Horse.*

1992
Portikus, Frankfurt. *Multiples 1964-1990.* Traveled to Lenbachhaus, Munich; Hochschule für angewandte Kunst, Vienna.

Cleveland Center for Contemporary Art, Cleveland, Ohio. *Recent Sculpture.*

Museum für Gegenwartskunst, Basel. *Die frühen Zeichnungen.*

Walker Art Center, Minneapolis. *In the Studio.*

In September 1994 the Guggenheim Museum and the Kunst- und Ausstellungshalle der Bundesrepublik Deutschland, Bonn, will present a major touring anthology of Oldenburg works to be presented in New York, Bonn, Paris, London, and Los Angeles.

Chronology of Performances

Snapshots from the City, Judson Gallery, New York, 1960

Blackouts, Reuben Gallery, New York, 1960

Ironworks / Fotodeath, Reuben Gallery, New York, 1961

Ray Gun Theater, The Store, 107 East Second Street, New York, 1961

> *Store Days I*
> *Store Days II*
> *Nekropolis I*
> *Nekropolis II*
> *Injun I*
> *Injun II*
> *Voyages I*
> *Voyages II*
> *World's Fair I*
> *World's Fair II*

Injun, Dallas, 1962

Sports, Green Gallery, New York, 1962

Gayety, University of Chicago, 1963

Stars, Washington Gallery of Modern Art, Washington, D.C., 1963

Autobodys, Los Angeles, 1963

Washes, Al Roon's Health Club, New York, 1965

Moveyhouse, New York, 1965

Massage, Moderna Museet, Stockholm, 1966

Il Corso del Coltello, (with Coosje van Bruggen and Frank O. Gehry), Venice, Italy, 1985

Sited Outdoor Works

Lipstick (Ascending) on Caterpillar Tracks, 1969-74
Cor-Ten, painted steel and aluminum, cast resin
24 x 11 x 13'
Yale University, Samuel Morse College, New Haven, Connecticut
[Originally sited in Beinecke Plaza, April 15, 1969;
resited in Samuel Morse College, October 17, 1974]

Three-Way Plug, 1969-73
Cor-Ten and bronze
9½ x 6½ x 4¾'
Oberlin College, Oberlin, Ohio (1/3)
St. Louis Museum of Art (2/3)
Private Collection, Wynnewood, Pennsylvania (3/3)

Giant Ice Bag, 1969
Steel, aluminum, cast resin, vinyl, wood, machinery
16½ x 18 x 18'
[First shown at 1970 World's Fair, Osaka, Japan. Also
shown at Los Angeles County Museum of Art; Dallas
Museum; Baltimore Museum; National Gallery of Art,
Washington, D.C.; and other venues]

Geometric Mouse, Scale A, 1965-75
Painted steel and aluminum
12 x 15 x 7'
Albany Mall, Albany, New York (Black — 1/6)
Southern Methodist University, Dallas (Black — 2/6)
Hirshhorn Museum and Sculpture Garden, Washington, D.C. (Black — 3/6)
Moderna Museet, Stockholm (yellow and blue — 4/6)
Walker Art Center, Minneapolis (yellow and blue — 5/6)
The Museum of Modern Art, New York (white — 6/6)

Geometric Mouse, Scale X, Red, 1971
Painted steel
18' high
Public Library, Houston
[Previously installed in Newport, Rhode Island; New York City]

Standing Mitt with Ball, 1973
12' high
Storm King Art Center, Mountainville, New York
[Previously installed at Wave Hill, Bronx, New York]

Alphabet / Good Humor, 1975
Painted fiberglass, resin and bronze
12 x 5⅔ x 2⅓'
Private collection, Chicago (1/2)
[Previously sited in private collection, Los Angeles]
Private collection, Berlin (2/2)

Colossal Ashtray, 1975
Lead, steel filled with urethane foam on steel base
6½ x 14½ x 13'
Neue Galerie — Sammlung Ludwig, Aachen, Germany
[First shown as part of touring exhibition *Oldenburg: Six Themes*; previously installed at Centre Georges Pompidou, Paris, and Nordjyllands Kunstmuseum, Aalborg, Denmark]

Inverted Q, 1976-1991
Painted Concrete, or resin
72 x 70 x 63"
Akron Art Institute, Akron, Ohio (Pink edition — 1/4)
Städtisches Museum Abteiberg, Mönchengladbach, Germany (Pink edition — 2/4)
Private collection, Santa Cruz, California (Pink edition — 3/4)
Samsung Corporation, Seoul, Korea (Pink edition, cast resin — 4/4)
Private collection, New York (Black edition, cast resin — 1/2)
Yokohama Museum, Japan (Black edition, cast resin — 2/2)
Collection of the artist (White, cast resin, trial proof)

Clothespin, 1976
Cor-Ten and stainless steel
45 x 6 x 4'
Centre Square, Philadelphia

Wayside Drainpipe, 1979
Cor-Ten, cement, found rocks
45' 8" x 8' 1" x 6' 6"
North Haven, Connecticut
[Previously installed on Doberman estate, Westphalia, Germany]

Tube Supported by its Contents, 1985
Painted bronze and steel
15' high
Lohausen Park, Düsseldorf

Knife Slicing Through Wall, 1989
Stainless steel, steel, stucco
Blade: 6 x 11½'
Margo Leavin Gallery, Los Angeles (1/2)

Monument to the Last Horse, 1991
Painted aluminum, urethane foam and resin
19½ x 17 x 12½'
Chinati Foundation, Marfa, Texas
[Previously installed at Seagram Plaza, New York]

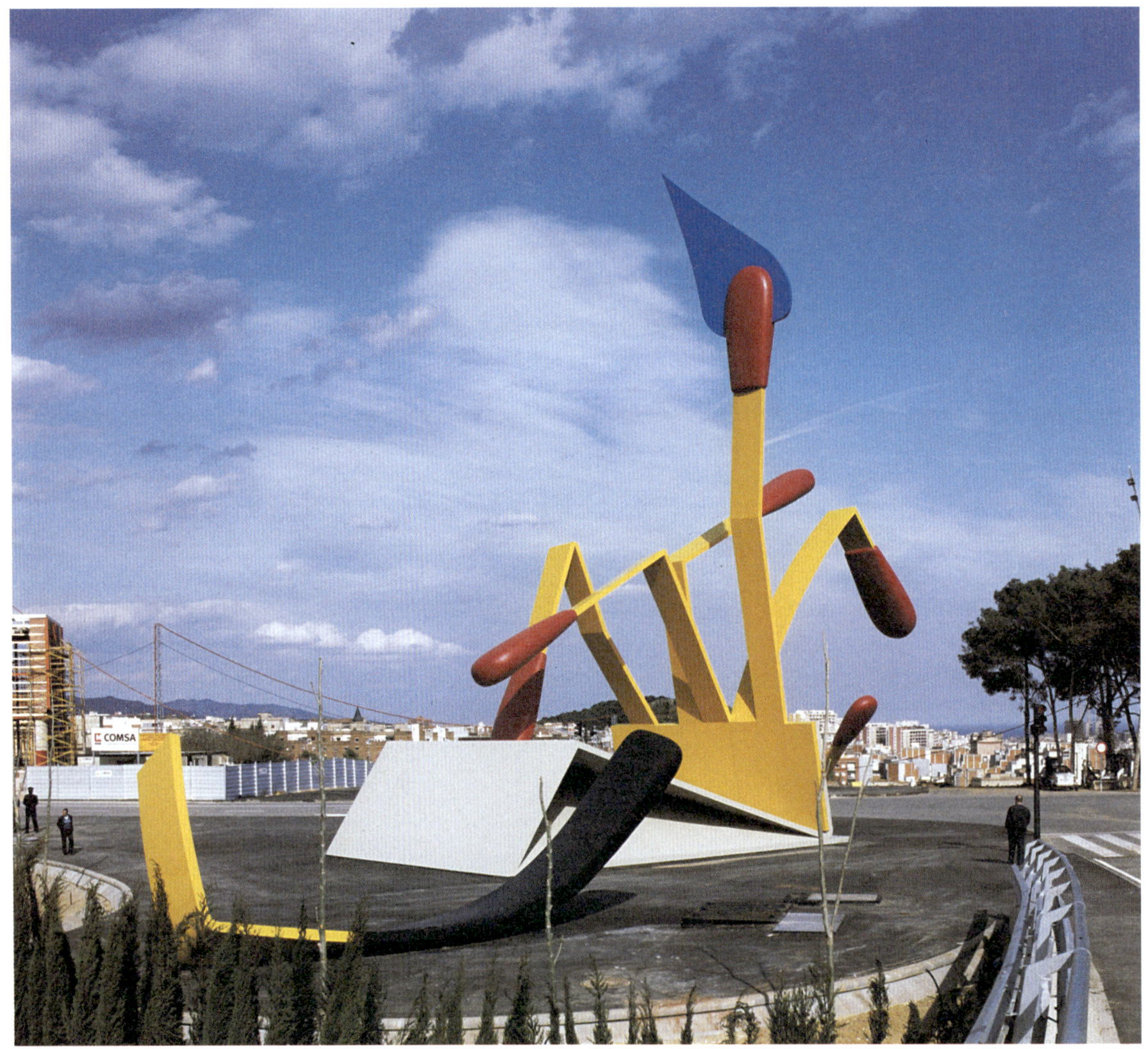

Mistos, 1992
painted steel, aluminum, fiberglass and resin
68' x 33' x 43' 4"
Vall d'Hebron, Barcelona

Large-Scale Projects with Coosje van Bruggen

1971-76
Giant Trowel I & II
Painted steel (blue)
38' 4½" [height]
Rijksmuseum Kröller-Müller, Otterlo, The Netherlands [November 1976] (I)
[Original version shown at *Sonsbeek 71*, Arnhem, The Netherlands 1971, later destroyed]

Painted steel (brown)
37' [height]
Pepsico Headquarters, Purchase, New York [July 1982] (II)

1977 / April
Batcolumn
Painted steel
100' 8" x 9' 6⅞"
Social Security Administration Building, Chicago

1977 / June
Pool Balls
Concrete
Three balls: 11' 6" in diameter each
Aaseeterrassen, Münster, Germany

1977 / November
Mouse Museum and Ray Gun Wing
Installed in Museum Moderner Kunst, Vienna, Austria, since 1980
[The collection of the *Mouse Museum* was first shown at *Documenta 5*, Kassel, Germany, 1972]

1978
Giant Switches
For the lobbies of the CBS Building, New York
Not realized

1979
Paintsplats (on a Wall by P.J.)
For façade of Marshall Field & Co., Houston
Not realized

1979 / November
Crusoe Umbrella
Painted steel
33' x 56' [height x length]
Civic Center, Des Moines, Iowa

1981 / March

Flashlight

Painted steel

38' 6" x 10' 6" x 10' 6"

University of Nevada, Las Vegas

1981 / June

Split Button

Painted aluminum

4' 11" x 16' x 16'

University of Pennsylvania, Philadelphia

1982 / March

Hat in Three Stages of Landing

Painted aluminum and steel

Three 'hats' each 9' 3" x 18' x 18'

[Each 'hat' is supported at different heights over a distance of 160']

Community Center, Salinas, California

1982 / April

Spitzhacke [Pick-Axe]

Painted steel

35' 5½" x 40' 4" [height x length]

Kassel, Germany

1983 / May

Gartenschlauch [Garden Hose]

Painted steel

36' high, length of 'hose', 410'

Stühlinger Park, Freiburg-im-Breisgau, Germany

1983 / June

Screwarch

Painted aluminum

12' 6" x 8' x 22' 6"

Museum Boymans-van Beuningen,
Rotterdam, The Netherlands

1983

Fishing Pole

Vail, Colorado

Not realized

1983 / November
Cross-section of a Toothbrush with Paste, in a Cup, on a Sink: Portrait of Coosje's Thinking
Painted aluminum and steel
19' 8" x 18' 1" x 17' 3"
Museum Haus Esters, Krefeld, Germany

1984 / April
Stake Hitch
Painted aluminum, steel, urethane foam, plastic materials
53' 6" x 15' 2" x 44' 6"
Dallas Museum of Art

1984 / May
Balancing Tools
Painted steel
Consisting of three 'tools' — 'hammer' 25' 11", 'screwdriver' 22' and 'pliers' 25' 6"
VITRA Factory, Weil-am-Rhein, Germany

1985-86
Coltello/Ship I & II [Knife/Ship]
(with Frank O. Gehry)
Wood, steel and plastic
35' 6" x 83' x 31' 10" (variable)
Originally made for the performance of *Il Corso del Coltello*, Venice, Italy, September 6, 1985
G.F.T, Torino, Italy (I)
The Museum of Contemporary Art, Los Angeles (II)

1985 / September
Toppling Ladder with Spilling Paint
Painted steel and aluminum
14' 2" [height]
Loyola Law School, Los Angeles

1988 / September
Spoonbridge and Cherry
Painted steel, aluminum, water
29' 6" x 51' 6" x 13' 6"
Walker Art Center, Minneapolis

1990 / March
Dropped Bowl, with Scattered Slices and Peels
Painted concrete, steel and other materials
15 parts covering an area of about 90' square
Open Space Park at Metro-Dade Government Center, Miami

1990 / November
Binoculars, part of *Chiat/Day/Mojo Offices* (with Frank O. Gehry)
Painted plaster, metal, various building materials
45' [height]
Venice, California

1990 / November
Free Stamp
Painted steel and aluminum
28 x 24 x 48'
Willard Park, Cleveland, Ohio

1990 / December
Bicyclette Ensevelie [Buried Bicycle]
Painted steel, aluminum, fiberglass
Four 'bicycle parts' of different dimensions in an
area of approximately 130' x 88' 6"
La Villette, Paris

1992 / January
Mistos [Match Cover]
Painted steel, aluminum, fiberglass and resin
68' x 33' x 43' 4"
Vall d'Hebron, Barcelona

Work in Progress

Bottle of Notes, to be completed in 1993
Painted steel
30' x 16' x 10'
Middlesbrough, England

Selected Group Exhibitions

1958
City Gallery, New York. *Drawings.*

1959
Judson Gallery, Judson Memorial Church, New York. *Judson Group: Baer, Dine, Oldenburg, Ratliff, Stasik, Tyler, Wesselman.*

Judson Gallery, Judson Memorial Church, New York. *Xmas Show: Drawings, Prints.*

Reuben Gallery, New York. *Below Zero.*

1960
Martha Jackson Gallery, New York. *New Forms — New Media.* [Parts I & II]

1961
Martha Jackson Gallery, New York. *Environments, Situations, Spaces.*

The Museum of Modern Art, New York. *Recent Acquisitions.*

1962
Dallas Museum for Contemporary Arts, Dallas. *1961.*

Sidney Janis Gallery, New York. *New Realists.*

Dwan Gallery, Los Angeles. *My Country 'Tis of Thee.*

1963
Allen Memorial Art Museum, Oberlin College, Oberlin, Ohio. *Three Young Americans.*

The Art Institute of Chicago, Chicago. *66th American Annual Exhibition.*

The Museum of Modern Art, New York. *Americans 1963.*

1964
Sidney Janis Gallery, New York. *4 Environments by 4 New Realists.*

Moderna Museet, Stockholm. *Amerikansk pop-konst.* Traveled to Louisiana Museum of Modern Art, Humlebaek, Denmark; Stedelijk Museum, Amsterdam.

Venice, Italy. *U.S. Representation, XXXII International Biennial Exhibition of Art: Four Germinal Painters-Four Younger Artists.*

Haags Gemeentemuseum, The Hague. *Nieuwe Realisten.* Traveled to Museum des 20. Jahrhunderts, Vienna; Akademie der Künste, Berlin; Palais des Beaux-Arts, Brussels.

Solomon R. Guggenheim Museum, New York. *American Drawings.*

1965
Solomon R. Guggenheim Museum, New York. *Eleven from the Reuben Gallery.*

1967
Art Gallery of Ontario, Toronto. *Dine, Oldenburg, Segal.* Traveled to Albright-Knox Art Gallery, Buffalo, New York.

Solomon R. Guggenheim Museum, New York. *Guggenheim International Exhibition 1967: Sculpture from 20 Nations.*

1968

Kassel, Germany. *Documenta 4.*

Museu de Arte Moderna, São Paulo. *São Paulo IX: Environment U.S.A. 1957-67.* Traveled to Brandeis University, Waltham, Massachusetts.

Richard Feigen Gallery, Chicago. *Richard J. Daley.*

1969

Vancouver Art Gallery, Vancouver. *New York 13.*

Sidney Janis Gallery, New York. *New Work by Seven Artists.*

Hayward Gallery, London. *Pop Art.*

The Metropolitan Museum of Art, New York. *New York Painting and Sculpture: 1940-1970.*

1970

United States Pavilion, Osaka, Japan. *Japan World Exposition, Osaka 1970: New Arts.*

1971

Los Angeles County Museum of Art, Los Angeles. *Art & Technology.*

1972

Kassel, Germany. *Documenta 5.*

1973

Moderna Museet, Stockholm. *New York Collection for Stockholm.*

1974

Whitney Museum of American Art, New York. *American Pop Art.*

Newport, Rhode Island. *Monumenta: Scale in Contemporary Sculpture.*

Dallas Museum of Fine Arts, Dallas, Texas. *Poets of the Cities, New York and San Francisco, 1950-1965.* Traveled to San Francisco Museum of Art, San Francisco; Wadsworth Atheneum, Hartford, Connecticut.

1975

Worcester Art Museum, Worcester, Massachusetts. *American Art Since 1945 from the Collection of The Museum of Modern Art.* Traveled to Toledo Museum of Art, Toledo, Ohio; Denver Art Museum, Denver; Fine Arts Gallery of San Diego, San Diego; Dallas Museum of Fine Arts, Dallas; Joslyn Art Museum, Omaha, Nebraska; Greenville County Museum of Art, Greenville, South Carolina; Virginia Museum of Fine Arts, Richmond, Virginia.

National Collection of Fine Arts, Smithsonian Institution, Washington, D.C. *Images of an Era: The American Poster 1945-1975.* Traveled to Corcoran Gallery of Art, Washington, D.C.; Contemporary Arts Museum, Houston; Museum of Science and Industry, Chicago; Grey Art Gallery and Study Center, New York University, New York.

1976

The Museum of Modern Art, New York. *Drawing Now.* Traveled to Kunsthalle, Zürich; Städtische Kunsthalle, Baden-Baden; Graphische Sammlung Albertina, Vienna; Sonia Henie-Niels Onstad Foundation, Oslo.

Solomon R. Guggenheim Museum, New York. *Twentieth Century American Drawing; Three Avant Garde Generations.* Traveled to Städtische Kunsthalle, Baden-Baden; Kunsthalle Bremen, Bremen, Germany.

The Art Institute of Chicago, Chicago. *Seventy-Second American Exhibition.*

Whitney Museum of American Art, New York. *200 Years of American Sculpture.*

Greenwich Arts Council, Greenwich, Connecticut. *Sculpture '76.*

Nassau County Museum of Art, Roslyn, New York. *Monuments and Monoliths: A Metamorphosis.*

1977

Kassel, Germany. *Documenta 6.*

Westfälisches Landesmuseum für Kunst und Kulturgeschichte, Münster, Germany. *Skulptur: Ausstellung in Münster.*

1980

Institute of Contemporary Art, University of Pennsylvania, Philadelphia. *Urban Encounters: Art, Architecture, Audience.*

Istituto di Cultura di Palazzo Grassi, Venice, Italy. *Pop Art: evoluzione di una generazione.*

1981

Museen der Stadt Köln, and Museum Ludwig, Cologne. *Westkunst: Zeitgenössische Kunst seit 1939.*

1982

Kassel, Germany. *Documenta 7.*

1983

Ceolfrith Gallery / Sunderland Arts Center, Sunderland, England. *Drawing in Air: An Exhibition of Sculptor's Drawings 1882-1982.*

Contemporary Arts Museum, Houston. *American Still Life 1945-1983.* Traveled to Albright-Knox Art Gallery, Buffalo, New York; Columbus Museum of Art, Columbus, Ohio; Neuberger Museum, State University of New York at Purchase, Purchase, New York; Portland Art Museum, Portland, Oregon.

Nassau County Museum of Art, Roslyn, New York. *Sculpture: The Tradition in Steel.*

1984

Whitney Museum of American Art, New York. *Blam! The Explosion of Pop, Minimal and Performance 1958-1964.*

1985

Art Gallery of New South Wales, Australia. *Pop Art 1955-70.* Traveled to Queensland Art Gallery, Queensland, Australia; National Gallery of Victoria, Sydney, Australia.

Smith College Museum of Art, Northampton, Massachusetts. *Dorothy C. Miller: With An Eye To American Art.*

Bruce Museum, Greenwich, Connecticut. *Sculpture: The Language of Scale.*

1986

Museum Haus Lange, Krefeld, Germany. *Vier Skulpturen und Graphische Werke aus dem Kaiser Wilhelm Museum Krefeld von: Beuys, Judd, Oldenburg und Serra.*

Leo Castelli Gallery, New York. *Kosuth, Morris, Oldenburg, Serra, Stella, Therrien.*

1987

University Art Museum, University of California at Berkeley, Berkeley. *Made in U.S.A.: An Americanization in Modern Art, The 50's and 60's.* Traveled to The Nelson-Atkins Museum of Art, Kansas City, Missouri; Virginia Museum of Fine Arts, Richmond, Virginia.

Margo Leavin Gallery, Los Angeles. *Sculpture of the Sixties.*

Institute of Contemporary Art, London. *Comic Iconoclasm.*

Centro Cultural Arte Contemporaneo, Mexico City. *Leo Castelli and His Artists: 30 Years of Promoting Contemporary Art.*

Centro de Arte Reina Sofía, Madrid. *The Sonnabend Collection.*

1988
The Museum of Modern Art, New York. *Committed to Print.*

Sidney Janis Gallery, New York. *60's /80's: Sculpture Parallels.*

Galerie Kaj Forsblom, Helsinki, Finland. *Celebrating Leo Castelli and Pop Art.*

The Museum of Modern Art, New York. *In Honor of Toiny Castelli: Drawings from the Toiny, Leo and Jean-Christophe Castelli Collection.*

1989
Musée national d'art moderne, Centre Georges Pompidou, and La Grande Halle, La Villette, Paris. *Magiciens de la Terre.*

1990
The Museum of Modern Art, New York. *High & Low: Modern Art and Popular Culture.* Traveled to The Art Institute of Chicago, Chicago; Museum of Contemporary Art, Los Angeles.

1991
Setagaya Art Museum, Tokyo. *Beyond the Frame: American Art 1960-1990.* Traveled to The National Museum of Art, Osaka, Japan; Fukuoka Art Museum, Fukuoka, Japan.

The Royal Academy of Art, London. *The Pop Art Show.* Traveled to Museum Ludwig, Cologne; Centro de Arte Reina Sofía, Madrid; Montreal Museum of Fine Arts, Montreal.

The Museum of Modern Art, New York. *For 25 Years: Gemini G.E.L.*

1992
Kunstmuseum, and Kunsthalle, Basel. *Transform: Bild Object Skulptur im 20. Jahrhundert.*

Solomon R. Guggenheim Museum, New York. *Masterpieces from the Collection.*

Museu Nacional de Belas Artes, Rio de Janerio. *...Reperti... O meio ambiente visto por 18 dos mais renomados artistas do mundo.*

Selected Bibliography

Gene Baro. *Claes Oldenburg: Drawings and Prints.* Lausanne: Publications I.R.L. (A Paul Bianchini Book); and London: Chelsea House Publishers, 1969.

Barbara Rose. *Claes Oldenburg.* New York: The Museum of Modern Art, 1970.

Barbara Haskell, with texts by the artist. *Claes Oldenburg: Object into Monument.* Pasadena Art Museum, 1971.

Ellen H. Johnson. *Claes Oldenburg.* New York: Penguin Books, 1971.

Götz Adriani, Dieter Koepplin, Barbara Rose. *Zeichnungen von Claes Oldenburg.* Basel: Kunstmuseum Basel; and Tübingen: Kunsthalle Tübingen, 1975.

Martin Friedman, and interview with the artist. *Oldenburg: Six Themes.* Minneapolis, Minnesota: Walker Art Center, 1975.

Coosje van Bruggen, Ad Petersen. *Claes Oldenburg: Tekeningen, aquarellen en grafiek.* Amsterdam: Stedelijk Museum, 1977; Paris: Musée national d'art moderne, Centre Georges Pompidou; Stockholm: Moderna Museet.

Coosje van Bruggen. *Claes Oldenburg: Mouse Museum / Ray Gun Wing.* Cologne: Museum Ludwig, 1979.

Coosje van Bruggen, Claes Oldenburg, R.H. Fuchs. *Claes Oldenburg: Large-Scale Projects, 1977-1980. A chronicle by Coosje van Bruggen & Claes Oldenburg, based on notes, statements, contracts, correspondence, and other documents related to the works.* New York: Rizzoli International Publications, Inc., 1980.

Cor Blok. *Claes Oldenburg: Het Schroefboog-projekt; een opdracht van Museum Boymans-van Beuningen, Rotterdam 1978-82. The Screwarch Project commissioned by Museum Boymans-van Beuningen, Rotterdam 1978-82.* Rotterdam, The Netherlands: Museum Boymans-van Beuningen, 1983.

Claes Oldenburg, Gerhard Storck. *Claes Oldenburg: Cross Section of a Toothbrush with Paste in a Cup on a Sink: Portrait of Coosje's Thinking.* Krefeld, Germany: Krefelder Kunstmuseen, 1985.

Claes Oldenburg, Coosje van Bruggen, Frank O. Gehry, Germano Celant. *El Cuchillo Barco, de Il Corso del Coltello.* Milan: Electa; and Madrid: Ministerio de Cultura, 1986.

Germano Celant, Coosje van Bruggen, Claes Oldenburg. *The Course of the Knife / Il Corso del Coltello.* Milan: Electa, 1986.

Gerhard Storck, Coosje van Bruggen. *The Haunted House.* Krefeld, Germany: Krefelder Kunstmuseen, 1987.

Germano Celant, Claes Oldenburg, Coosje van Bruggen. *A Bottle of Notes and Some Voyages.* Sunderland: Northern Centre for Contemporary Art; Leeds: The Henry Moore Centre for the Study of Sculpture, Leeds City Art Galleries; New York: Rizzoli International Publications, Inc., 1988.

Coosje van Bruggen. *Claes Oldenburg: Dibujos / Drawings 1959-1989.* Valencia, Spain: IVAM, Instituto Valenciano de Arte Moderno, 1989.

Coosje van Bruggen. *Claes Oldenburg: Nur ein anderer Raum.* Frankfurt: Museum für Moderne Kunst, 1991.

Arthur Solway, Thomas Lawson, Claes Oldenburg, David Platzker. *Claes Oldenburg: Multiples in Retrospect, 1964-1990.* New York: Rizzoli International, 1991.

Martin Hentschel, Thomas Lawson, David Platzker. *Claes Oldenburg: Multiples 1964-1990.* Frankfurt: Portikus, 1992

Dieter Koepplin. *Claes Oldenburg: Die frühen Zeichnungen.* Basel: Museum für Gegenwartskunst, 1992.

Selected Books by the Artist

Store Days. New York, Villefranche-sur-mer, Frankfurt am Main: Something Else Press, Inc; 1967.

Claes Oldenburg, interview with the artist by Paul Carroll. *Proposals for Monuments and Buildings 1965-69.* Chicago: Big Table Publishing Company, 1969.

Claes Oldenburg, Constructions, Models, and Drawings. Chicago, Richard Feigen Gallery, 1969.

Notes in Hand. Petersburg Press, 1971.

Raw Notes. Halifax, Nova Scotia, Canada: The Press of the Nova Scotia College of Art and Design, 1973.

Claes Oldenburg and Coosje van Bruggen. *Sketches and Blottings Toward The European Desk Top.* Milan and Turin: Galleria Christian Stein; and Florence: Hopeful Monster, 1990

Selected Films

Sort of a Commercial for an Ice Bag. Directed by Michel Hugo. Cinematography by Eric Saarinen. Edited by John Hoffman. Sound by Howard Chesley. 16mm color film with sound, 30 minutes. Produced by Gemini G.E.L., Los Angeles, 1970.

Claes Oldenburg. Edited by Lana Jokel. Cinematography by Nicholas Proferes. Additional cinematography by Christian Blackwood and Seth Schneidman. Sound by James Musser. Production Manager: Stephen Westheimer. 16mm color film with sound, 52 minutes. Produced by Blackwood Productions, Inc., New York, 1973-74.

School Bus Yellow / Adirondack Green. Directed and produced by Coosje van Bruggen and Machteld Schrameijer. Cinematography by Francis Freedland, Jesper Sorensen, and Vibeke Winding. Sound by Robert Ghiraldini. Edited by Donald George Klocek. Music by Al Scotti. 16mm color film with sound, 49 minutes. Distributed by Store Days Inc., New York, 1982.

Claes Oldenburg / Coosje van Bruggen: Large-Scale Projects. Produced, directed and edited by Lana Jokel and Nick Doob. Cinematography by Nick Doob. 16mm color film with sound, 56 minutes. Distributed by Lana Jokel, New York, 1991.

Awards

Brandeis Award for Sculpture, 1971

Skowhegan Medal for Sculpture, 1972

1st Prize Sculpture, 72nd American Exhibition,
The Art Institute of Chicago, 1976

Medal of the American Institute of Architects, 1977

Wilhelm-Lehmbruck Sculpture Award, Duisburg, Germany, 1981

Wolf Foundation Prize in Visual Arts, Israel, 1989

Memberships

American Academy and Institute of Arts and Letters, 1975

American Academy of Arts and Sciences, 1978

Public Collections

The Art Institute of Chicago
Carnegie Museum of Art, Pittsburgh
Centre national d'art et de culture Georges Pompidou, Paris
Chinati Foundation, Marfa, Texas
Dallas Museum
Hirshhorn Museum and Sculpture Garden, Washington, D.C.
IVAM Centre Julio González, Valencia, Spain
Kunstmuseum Basel
Los Angeles County Museum of Art
Moderna Museet, Stockholm
Museum für Moderne Kunst, Frankfurt
Museum Ludwig, Cologne
Museum of Contemporary Art, Chicago
Museum of Contemporary Art, Los Angeles
The Museum of Modern Art, New York
National Gallery of Art, Washington, D.C.
Neue Galerie — Sammlung Ludwig, Aachen, Germany
Philadelphia Museum of Art
Rijksmuseum Kröller-Müller, Otterlo, The Netherlands
San Francisco Museum of Modern Art
Solomon R. Guggenheim Museum, New York
Stedelijk Museum, Amsterdam
Tate Gallery, London
Walker Art Center, Minneapolis
Whitney Museum of American Art, New York

This exhibition is dedicated to Coosje van Bruggen, whose interests and experiences, especially in relation to Paris (a city she taught me not to fear) form the actual subjects of the works.

C.O.

Photography of art work by Ellen Page Wilson
Photograph of Claes Oldenburg by Ad Petersen
Photograph of *Mistos* by Claes Oldenburg

Cover:
Soft Saxophone, Scale A, Muslin, 1992, (Detail)
muslin, hardware cloth, urethane foam, wood, dacron and latex paint
11¼ x 27 x 49"

Endpapers:
Notebook Page: Studies for Leaf Boat Cargo and Perfume Bottles, 1991, (Detail)
pencil
11 x 8½"

Biographic & bibliographic histories by David Platzker

Catalogue designed and produced by Pace Publications

Assistants in fabrication of art work:
Celeste Livingston, John Franklin, James (Lord) Byron,
Don & Alfred Lippincott, and the crew of Lippincott Inc.,
North Haven, Connecticut

Library of Congress Catalog Card Number: 92-61388
ISBN: 1-878283-25-1

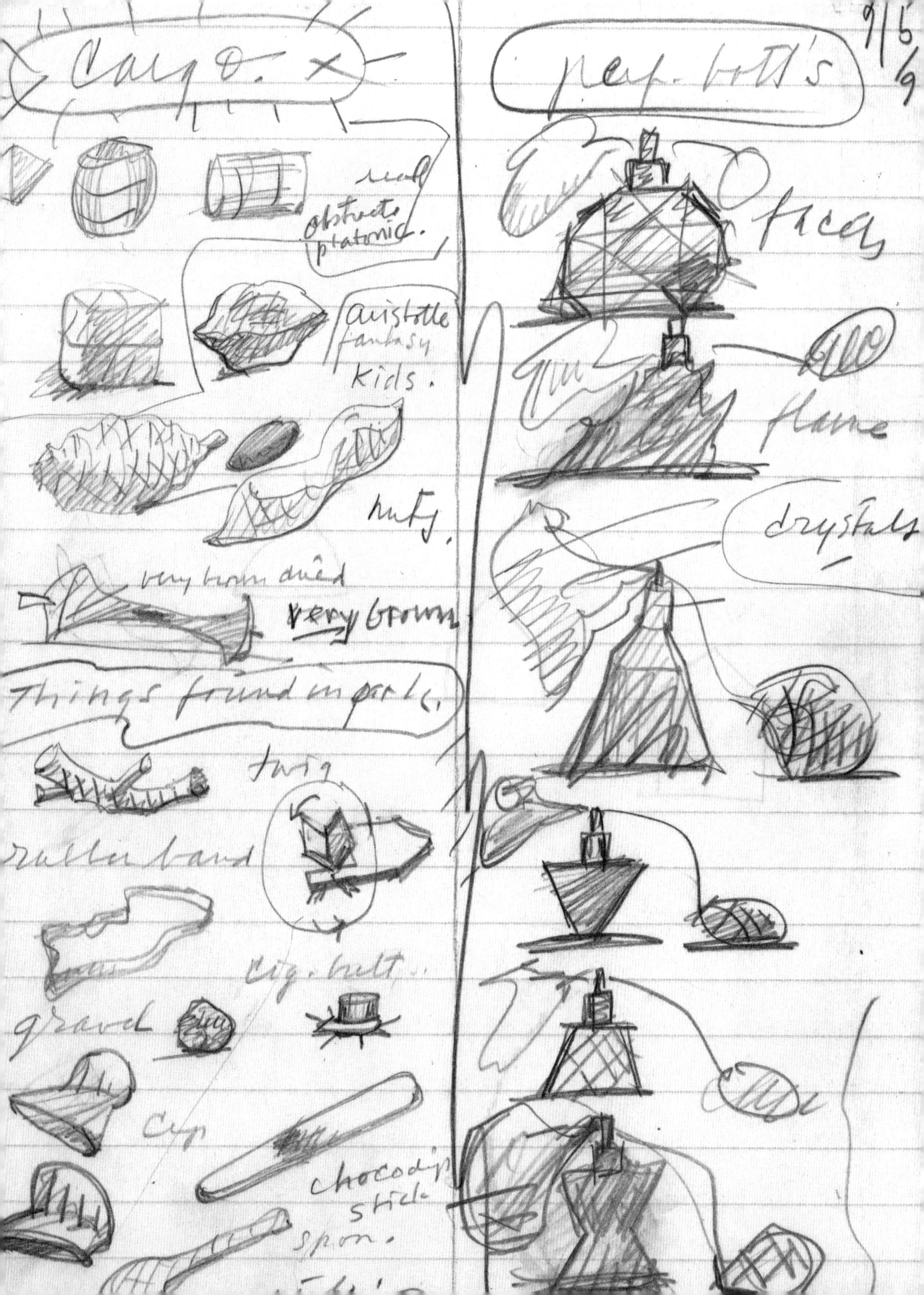

cargo. ×

real abstracts platonic.

aristotle fantasy kids.

nuts.

very brown dried

very brown.

Things found in park.

twig

rubber band

cig. butt.

gravel

cup

chocodip stick

spoon.

pap. bott's

9/5/9

tree

flame

crystals

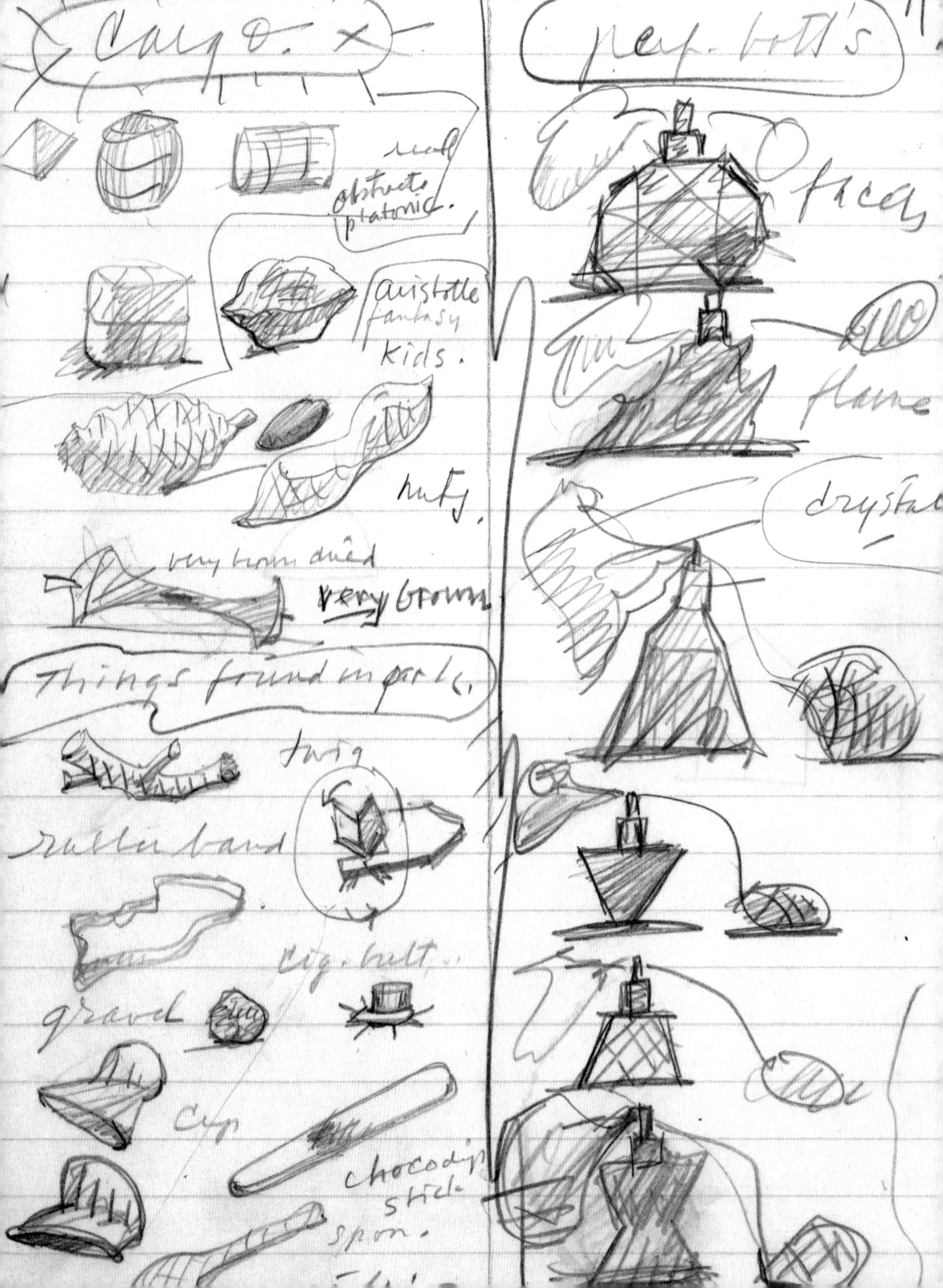

cargo. ×

small
abstracts
platonic.

aristotle
fantasy
kids.

nuts.

very brown dried

very brown

Things found in park.

twig

rubber band

cig. butt.

gravel

cup

chocodip
stick

spoon.

pep. bott's

faces

flame

crystal